THE
LOVE *of a* FATHER
AND THE
JOURNEY *of* HIS PRODIGAL SON

The LOVE *of a* FATHER

My son,
I love you and from the beginning,
I have selected you to tell others about how much
I have done for you. Use well the opportunities I give you.
I will use you and your testimony to reach multitudes of people.
Though you feel like you have wasted your young adult life,
I will use you in a mighty way to bear witness about Me and what
I have done for you. You are and will be a messenger of my word.
Don't be afraid because I am with you. You only have to
follow me and do what I tell you to do and remember
that in perseverance and
patience the victory is won.

– Unknown Author

The LOVE *of a* FATHER

THE
LOVE *of a* FATHER
AND THE
JOURNEY *of* HIS PRODIGAL SON

written by **MARCUS CLAPPER**

F I R S T   E D I T I O N
Published in 2021

Written by: Marcus Clapper | www.**WeAreTheProdigal**.com |
7521 Paula Drive, P.O. Box 262767, Tampa, FL 33685
ISBN: 978-1-7371817-0-5

Library of Congress Control
Clapper, Marcus
The Love of a Father and the Journey of His Prodigal Son
Control Number: 1-10063111271 | January, 2021

Library of Congress Cataloging-in-Publication Data
Category: Christian Living, Autobiography, Motivational & Inspirational
Cover Design & Formatting by: Eli Blyden | www.EliTheBookGuy.com
Edited by: The Writing Professor | www.TheWritingProfessor.com
Published & Printed in the United States of America | Tampa, Florida

Dedication

I wholly dedicate *The Love of a Father and the Journey of His Prodigal Son* to God who is my heavenly Father and Jesus Christ who is my eternal savior. I praise God every day for His mercy and grace and for saving a sinner like me from physical and spiritual death. I would not be alive today if it were not for His patience, mercy, and forgiveness. My prayer is that I honor Him with my life and my story, of which He is the author and creator.

I dedicate this book to my earthly father. Dad, I am eternally grateful for your love and the sacrifices you have made for my life. The pain we share unites us on earth, and more importantly, in heaven. We are stronger for the challenges we have faced together and we would not have the love and relationship we have today if it were not for our shared challenges. On Father's Day, twenty years ago, when I called you from jail to tell you I had been arrested, I never thought that our relationship, which was filled with anger and bitterness and was virtually non-existent at that time, could be repaired. I could not imagine at that time that we would ever be a part of each other's lives the way we are today. I owe so much of who I am to you. I love you, Dad.

I also dedicate this book to my loving, forgiving, and eternally patient wife, Michelle. You have been supportive and remained by me when many would not and most did not. You have seen a light in me that many haven't, and that many times, almost went out. I love you for your mercy and forgiveness. Most of all, I am thankful that I had you by my side especially during the hard times.

I cannot imagine we would have made it without each other. I love you, Michelle!

☙

I dedicate this book to my mom, Brenda, and my sister, Evonne. We have been through so much together and your love and support has never waned. You have both been a blessing to our family and me in so many ways. I love you, both.

☙

Lastly, I dedicate this book to my children, Michael and Mykala. You might never fully understand your purpose for my life, but God sent you both to save me and that is exactly what you did. My prayer is that your light shines brighter than mine ever will and that God will always come first in every aspect of your lives. So many times, when I thought I could not muster the strength to continue on, you have been the joy that has kept me going. I love you both more than I ever thought possible. I will always be there for you no matter what. *I love you forever,* Daddy

Table of Contents

Foreword

❧

Everybody has a story. Some may seem uneventful, others dramatic, while others are life changing. This story, Marcus' story, is a life changer.

Sometimes in life, people veer off course and are not always aware of how they had gotten so far away from what is good, true, and right. Nevertheless, God knows when things are not right, and if we allow Him, He will take the wrong in all of our lives and make it right. Though this is not my story, I was a player in the events. As a player, when my son called me from jail on Father's Day of 2000 and gave me an ultimatum to either stand by him and love him unconditionally from that moment forward or to never be a part of his life again, the decision marked a pivotal moment in our relationship. We would finally let each other back into our lives— all I had to do was love him. Although I had not stopped loving him, I also had not told or showed him my love, the love of a father, since he was a boy. Many years had passed and now he was a twenty-five-year-old man seeking my unconditional love. It was time to see that we both needed to change before it was too late.

God heals the broken and broken-hearted; He loves those who feel unloved if only we will let Him. To discover the power of authentic forgiveness and grace, read on in *The Love of a Father and the Journey of His Prodigal Son*. Forgiveness rewrites the future of all our stories! May God be glorified by using this story to speak to that unloved child or that parent who has walked away from the most important facets of their child's (children's) life. Marcus, thank you for being a vessel that God will continue to use.

Love,
Your Dad, Dale

The LOVE *of a* FATHER

Preface

～

In May of 2015, God started laying on my heart that I should write a book about my journey through life. This completely caught me off guard. I had so many questions. Why would God impress upon me to write a book? Who would want to read about my life? God, what could I possibly have to offer others? I repeatedly inquired of God to learn His purpose behind what seemed like a daunting task. I wrestled with the idea and tried to understand God's purpose. After all, I was not an author nor a public speaker nor a famous athlete, so I wondered, why would the public be interested in reading a book I wrote? I asked God, "Who really wants to read about me?" Yet, deep within, I knew exactly what God wanted. I knew what He was asking me to do.

Fifteen years earlier, God saved me from a life without freedom. He saved me from a life that would not have included the family that I love so dearly, and on several occasions, He saved me from death itself. Miraculously, God had saved me from a future life I cannot fathom living today. In the years that followed, I had mentioned to those who knew about my past that I would someday use my story to help others. I never knew what form that help would take or when that day would come, but when the words came out of my mouth, I knew it would happen.

So, here I was fifteen years later, and the time had finally come for me to put my words into action. *My* problem with God's plan is that my life had changed dramatically in the past fifteen years. During that time, so many positive changes had happened to me. I had gotten married to my wife Michelle in October 2000. Also, during this time, after a long battle, I was finally able to free myself of addiction. In 2005, I had gone back to college to further my education and become a CPA. In 2010, we had children and I became a stay at home parent. We have always loved to travel and had been blessed with the financial freedom to do this regularly. Michelle had just made partner at her firm and the financial blessings that our family enjoyed were growing exponentially. So many positive and amazing things had happened in my life over the past fifteen years and I had become extremely comfortable with my current lot in life, and I was not certain I cared to shake it up in any way. For weeks, I wrestled with the task to write a book—a task I believe God assigned.

Finally, I decided to share this with my wife to get her take on the matter. Secretly, I was hoping she would laugh at me and dissuade me from doing it, which was part of my motivation for sharing with her. I was hoping she would laugh at the thought of me writing a book and tell me the idea was ridiculous so when God asked me to write it again, I could blame my decision not to write the book on her. She would be the perfect scapegoat. I remember first sharing with her what God was laying on my heart while we were in Puerto Rico on a trip without our kids for a long weekend. On our first day, we were lying on the beach chatting. We were both feeling nice and relaxed so I sprang it on her. I shared how I had been hearing God tell me to put my life story in writing. I waited for her to laugh and completely blow the idea off, but her response was exactly what I expected from her. True to her form, she was supportive and encouraged me to follow through with what I was hearing. She was as solid and predictable as ever. Ugh! Now, what was I going to do? I knew that I could not count on Michelle to help me get out of writing my book, so I had to figure out a way to get out of it on my own.

In the book of Jonah in the Bible, God commanded Jonah to go to Nineveh to warn the residents of their sin and the destruction it would bring if they did not repent. Jonah believed that the people of Nineveh would harm him for this message. Jonah's fear of what would happen to him and a strong sense of self-preservation caused him to run from God instead of obeying Him. Jonah decided to take passage on a boat sailing to Tarshish, which was in the opposite direction from where God had commanded him to go. Jonah thought he could run from God. So, God used a vicious storm and three days in the belly of a large fish to convince Jonah to follow His directions. I was now faced with what seemed like a decision that was equally as daunting as the one Jonah had faced. God was instructing me to do something that I knew would be life changing and would force me out of the comfortable life I was living. The unknown of what God was asking me caused me great fear and anxiety. So, in the truest nature of Jonah, I did what I had always done best. I decided it was time to run the other way. I thought I could run from God. So, that is exactly what I did. I ran and ignored God for as long and as hard as I could. I tried to ignore God's voice by focusing my time on my health, my family, traveling, sports, and pretty much anything else that would serve as a good distraction. I focused all of my attention on me and how I wanted to live my life. This only made the "voice in my head" telling me to write a book get louder. As I tried to make excuse after excuse for why I could not and would not write this book, the voice kept getting louder and louder. In His own way, God visited me like he visited Jonah. Finally, I realized that running from God did not silence His command, but amplified it. As Jonah believed he was safe on the ship to Tarshish, I also believed I was safe in my running. I then realized my running was not working and that the Holy Spirit was not going to disappear until I started acting obediently.

I was motivated and quickly wrote my story. I felt a great sense of accomplishment. For the first time in a long time, I had put my mind to a project and had seen it through. I felt a peace that I had never felt before. This was an entirely new feeling for me. This was the peace that comes from hearing God's command for your life and doing what He asks in total obedience. If you have experienced this peace, you know exactly what I'm talking about. Life was calm in every way. Waking up in the morning was enjoyable and not a burden. It was God's peace flowing through me and enveloping every part of me.

My next steps were to share my story. I wasn't entirely clear what this would look like, so I met with a former pastor of mine and shared my story with him. He was truly blown away with what I shared from my past and how far I had come. He suggested having my story published into a book and since he had published multiple books of his own, he had a publisher that he put me in contact with. I reached out to this publisher and started moving in this direction. The ball was finally rolling. The peace that I could sense was a constant reminder that I was heading in the right direction. In the midst of my efforts to start working with a publisher to share my story, out of nowhere, I heard another voice. This voice sounded differently and had a different message. This voice was the voice of fear and insecurity. It reminded me that there were people from my past who might not want me to write about what had happened. There were also people from my past who would potentially attempt to harm my family and myself. This voice reminded me that Michelle had a great career and that our past could possibly ruin it all. I did not identify the voice immediately, but the only way I can describe how it made me feel is that all the peace that I had been feeling while I was following God's path was gone. This voice did not bring peace. It brought anxiety and fear. I felt uneasy with the direction of my life. I didn't sleep well and I felt chaos in many parts of my life. As I felt God's peace slip farther away, I realized that this was the voice of Satan.

Satan's tactics and his message worked and I ran away—again. This time even harder as I allowed the fear and insecurity to rise up within me. I allowed the terror of my past to, once again, grip my life. I told God that I was not ready. I remember saying, "Hey God, love the plan and all, but I'm not sure this is such a good idea. Maybe you have the wrong guy?" I did what I had done for the past fifteen years. I hid. I once again buried my head in my health and my family. I made excuses for why I couldn't continue. I told God that I didn't feel well and had to focus on that before finishing. I explained to Him that if I didn't feel well, how was I supposed to focus on what He wanted me to communicate. Our family travels quite a bit, so I would tell God that as soon as we get back from the next trip I'll buckle down and get this done. But when the time came for me to make good on my word, I would point to the next trip and say I have too much on my plate right now to finish the process of completing my story. Ironically, each trip was never as much fun or as relaxing as I had envisioned it would be prior to going as there was always this weight hanging over my head. I always told God that I needed to focus on what is right in front of me. I constantly made a list of all the things I needed to accomplish and would always put "finish my story" at the bottom of that list. Not surprisingly, it always transferred to the next list and ended up on the bottom. I boarded my own personal boat to Tarshish, just like Jonah did, and tried to put my book and God's plans for my life in the rear-view mirror.

Not surprisingly, the chaos in my life started to become greater and more noticeable. Over time, God again started tugging on my heart and my mind. He started to speak to me again and eventually I started listening. He reminded me that He is the God of everything.

He has given me all that I have, and He only asks me to be obedient in return. God reminded me that my story was intended to be shared with others with the hope of saving just one life and this could not happen if I did not follow His plan.

I wish I could say that that was the last time I ran from God. As I write this, over five years later, and after God started telling me to start this project, I have started and stopped writing several times. Every time I pick up the manuscript and say I am going to cross the finish-line, I immediately sense a peace and wisdom that is not of my own. Then, something happens that distracts me or makes me question what I am doing. These distractions always come in different shapes and sizes. I, again, became distracted by my health or my family and would convince myself there was just not enough time in the day to do this. I would say I feel too tired to spend an hour or two a day on my story, but I am never too tired to spend an hour or two a day at the gym. So, I again pushed the pause button. Ironically, every time I get distracted and allow myself to "put it on hold," one or more parts of my life seems to feel chaotic and unsettled. I then begin to hear that voice grow louder again.

It is in these times, that I am constantly reminded that the enemy does not want me to share my story. God reminds me that the message I have to share of hope, love, and forgiveness is one that the world and those around me need to hear. I have finally realized that the story I must tell is not my story to decide what to do with; it is God's story and He will get all the glory and decide the direction that it takes.

Introduction

∾

*T*he Love of a Father and the Journey of His Prodigal Son has been fifteen years in the making. Many times, when I have sought God in a time of silence, I have asked Him what He wants to accomplish from the publishing of this book. I am curious to see what His plan looks like for my life and what to expect from this journey He has set me upon. I sat, still and quiet, waiting to hear God's response, but I heard silence. I have realized that the silence does not mean He is not listening or that He has no plan. From Jeremiah 29:11, I am reminded that He has a plan for my life; plans to give me hope, a future, and His expected end. By spending time in prayer, I have learned to be patient and obedient. He is waiting for my complete obedience in this project in order to surprise me with His plan. Because He reveals as we are obedient to His commands, I know He will reveal His plan to me in His time, kind of like a present at Christmas. God *loves* surprises! Just ask my wife when we found out she was pregnant, and then a week later, finding out we were having twins. Surprise!

Other times, when I ask God what He wants to accomplish, I do not hear silence. Instead, I hear Him asking,

"Marcus, what do you want to accomplish from writing this book?"

"Isn't it obvious God? I want to use my past to help others with their pain and struggles their past or present has created for them. God, I want to save as many lives as I can" is generally *my response.*

My response sounds humble on the surface, but I was never comfortable with it or sure I was being honest. Over the five years since God laid on my heart to write this book, I realized that I was wrestling with pride and the need for recognition for me being freed from addiction, escaping death on multiple occasions, and not being in jail for most, if not, all of my life. Sure, I would say the right things and know in my heart that I wanted to do the right things, but I was still allowing pride to fuel part of my motivation to complete this book. Once I recognized this, I had to honestly ask myself, "Am I doing this for God's kingdom or am I doing this for Marcus' kingdom?"

In my heart, I knew the answer. I knew some part of me was seeking approval and validation from the world around me. I could sense that I was seeking others to read my story and praise me for overcoming the circumstances I had created and for eventually forging an impossible path of freedom, success, and deliverance from addiction for my life. I wanted part and all of the credit for what I had done with my life and what I had become, when really, the only parts I deserved credit for were the mistakes I had made along the way. If I had been left to my own devices, I would be in jail or even worse—dead.

God laid on my heart that in order for me to share the message I was intended to share, my pride had to be dealt with; I needed to work diligently on humility and being humble with what I have been given. So, I repeatedly laid my pride at the feet of God and asked for a humble spirit. And He has answered many times over. Sure, this process has been painful at times. I have been stubborn and God's way of humbling me has not always been how I was expecting or wanting to be humbled. Yet, through the pain of His process, I have gained a greater appreciation for my journey and for His plan. I now realize why God allowed over five years to pass between the start of this project and the completion of this project.

I was not ready.

So, now when I hear that voice ask me what I want to accomplish from telling my story. The answer is clear to me. God, allow for just one life to be saved. As I humble myself before God, I realize that all I want from my story is to be able to help one person. I just want one person who is feeling the pain of their past or present to be able to relate to some aspect of my story and see the hope in his or her life.

There have been many times in my past I did not see that hope or light in myself. Many times, I felt broken and ashamed. I have felt unlovable and flawed because of my mistakes. I cannot even count the number of times I have wanted to give up—I felt helpless and hopeless. I have told myself repeatedly that the things I have done in my past are unforgiveable. I have repeated and believed the lie that my family and God cannot and will not forgive me. I allowed fear, insecurity, and depression to become my way of life, never believing that love, joy, and peace were possible. I convinced myself of these lies; I believed them for years and finally decided that I would never forgive myself. For many years, I wrestled with, and was tormented by, these beliefs. It was a battle I was losing and almost lost.

When I listen to what many people in the world around me are saying, I hear so many of them saying these same things. I hear people say that their past cannot be forgiven by God or those closest to them. These people say, "if you only knew what I had done..." I have been told by many that you cannot be arrested for significant crimes and then have success in life. I have heard parents say that their son and/or daughter committed a "stupid" crime at a young age and they think that they cannot go back to school or get a job in the white-collar world because of their past. The parents hurt for their child because they see them stuck in unforgiveness and depression. In the news and through the media and social media, we see and hear anger, chaos, and brokenness everywhere. People hate those that disagree with them and are using anger, violence and chaos, which are authored by Satan, as a tool to retaliate against those they disagree with, while championing what they claim to be peace, love and unity. Our world and the minds and souls of many in it are broken. I see a world that needs hope and has allowed so many lies and distractions to block their hope.

As we all look at our lives and question the things that we have done and listen to the lies that we are telling ourselves or allowing ourselves to believe, I am reminded of what Apostle Paul wrote in 1 Timothy 1:15-16.

> "This is a trustworthy saying, and everyone should accept it: "Christ Jesus came into the world to save sinners"—and I am the worst of them all. But God had mercy on me so that Christ Jesus could use me as a prime example of his great patience with even the worst sinners. Then others will realize that they, too, can believe in him and receive eternal life."

Apostle Paul was one of the greatest men of the Christian faith the world has ever known, but he was also responsible for the torture and death of countless Christians before he came to Christ. 1 Timothy 1:15-16 shows that Paul was able to fully accept God's forgiveness for his past. He realized that even though he had committed great sin against God and God's people, he could allow himself to be used to spread God's message of eternal salvation, unconditional love, and forgiveness no matter what he had done. God used Paul, not despite of his past, but *because* of his past. So, after many years of saying I was going to be obedient, but letting my past get in the way, I finally drew a line in the sand and said enough is enough. I finally chose to use 1 Timothy 1:15-16 as a benchmark for my life and not a reminder of my sin and past. I chose to finally release myself of the unforgiveness of my past and allow myself to be used in the manner that God has intended.

I want you to understand that neither God, my parents, or anyone else, for that matter, forced me to make the bad choices I made. So, as you read through my story, do not think that I am in any way placing blame on others or downplaying my responsibility for my actions. Quite the opposite. I am simply trying to paint a realistic picture of how I felt as a teenager and young adult. I am doing this because I know there are teenagers and young adults who will read this who feel the same way. Conversely, there will be parents who read my story who have also made mistakes or are raising teenagers and young adults who rebelled just as I did and are trying to figure out what to do and how to handle them.

In *The Love of a Father and the Journey of His Prodigal Son*, I retell my life's journey from the beginning until now and the challenges with my relationship with my dad and God and a life of sin and addiction. I share how I was saved from a life in prison and the many challenges I faced after escaping that fate. In the first chapter, I discuss how all men and women are created equal in sin and how all of our screw ups might feel different, but really are not. I also discuss the final wakeup call I needed to start letting go of my past. In the second chapter, I take ownership for my actions from start to finish. This is extremely important for me to overcome and I talk about how I finally accepted responsibility for my actions. In the third chapter, I walk through my early life. I talk about my family and the environment I was raised in and what my version of God looked like. The fourth chapter talks about my teenage years and how my relationship with my family, most significantly my dad, and with God began to deteriorate. My first arrest in college and the ways in which my life spiraled out of control in college comprises the fifth chapter. I also discuss my life away from my parents and how my and Michelle's relationship began to fall apart. In the sixth chapter, I share the ways in which I became involved in consuming and selling drugs. I share my transition from selling a few drugs each night in clubs to selling large amounts of drugs out of state. You will learn of a life without boundaries that looked great on the surface, but had created a mess in my relationship with my family and God. In the seventh chapter, I describe how one phone call changed my life forever. Chapter eight is the heart of my journey. I retell how I was arrested in June 2000 and the events that happened in the months that followed. Here, I share the three significant events that God used to save me from a life in prison and to write a story for Michelle and I's lives that could never have been possible without God's hand of direction and protection. In chapter nine, I discuss the challenges that I faced after my arrest, which included battling depression and addiction and my sentencing and finally coming "home" to my dad and receiving and accepting his love for me in chapter ten. Returning to God was not easy. I describe how I relented and returned to Him in chapter eleven as well as the depression, self-doubt, and unforgiveness I had toward myself that held me in bondage for many years. I also talk about my life's journey in my early thirties. Chapter twelve is about what God used to finally get my attention to follow His path for my life and stop stumbling over my own poor choices. I describe the two people that God miraculously brought into my life to save me for the last time. Finally, in chapter thirteen, I summarize how my relationship with my dad and God paralleled each other. I talk about my dad being there for me when neither of us thought that would be possible and yet, it happened.

As you read *The Love of a Father and the Journey of His Prodigal Son*, my prayer is that you are able to fully understand what God's mercy, grace, and forgiveness look like. I pray that you are able to relate some part of this story to your own and be able to use it to transform your life. My prayer is that you fully understand that

I am just a stay at home dad, no one special, or unique. I am just a guy who made poor choices and had to face the consequences of those choices. My pain and past are no different from anyone else's. Yes, it may sound and look different, but all of our sins are the same in that they are forgivable and forgiven if we ask. I want you to see how a father and son, who hadn't spoken or shown love to each other for many, many years, could forgive each other and love and respect each other with open arms. I also want you to understand how my relationship with my father mirrored my relationship with God and how both my earthly father and my Heavenly Father were waiting for me when I finally decided to come back to them. It turned out they had loved me the whole time, but I didn't see or understand that. I also want you to see how even after all the mistakes I made, I was still able to be successful with my life. No, it wasn't easy. I faced many hurdles both internally and externally along the way. But I always had hope. I never let go of the hope that someday things could be different. Even in my darkest hour, I still held onto the hope that change would come. For me, that change came slowly and it was painful. But I have learned that from my pain others can and will find hope. My prayer is that those I have hurt along the way or wronged in any way, and there are many, would forgive me for turning my back on them or for hurting them in any way. My prayer is that you will see and feel love in this book; the kind of love that does not have conditions attached or judgement or that would tear others down. This is the love between a son and his parents that seemed lost, but was found. This is the love between a boyfriend and a girlfriend, who became a husband and a wife, and who went through so much together that no one except them will ever understand or know about; they never turned their backs on each other and always stood by each other no matter what. This is the love between a father and his children whose birth and lives have changed their father's life forever. I pray that someday they will read this and be able to use this in their darkest hour and know that I will stand by them and love them no matter what.

Most importantly, I hope you see the love between our Heavenly Father and his prodigal son who turned his back on his Father. But no matter what, God always loved me and was always there for me. Many times, it didn't feel like it, but like footprints in the sand, He was there. I just wasn't looking for or listening to Him. I am thankful for God's mercy, patience, and grace for me. I am thankful for every moment of every day that I have because there was a time when I didn't think I would have them. Lastly, my prayer is that you will understand that my sin and the guilt and pain it has caused will no longer be victorious in my life. I wrote *The Love of a Father and the Journey of His Prodigal Son* because I want just one person to know that their sin and the guilt and pain it has caused them does not have to be victorious in their life either.

CHAPTER 1

For All Have Sinned....

∽

God, the God of Adam, Abraham, David, Paul, and each and every one of us, can do all things. He is all powerful and omnipotent. He created all things before me, including the heavens, earth, and stars in the sky. This alone proclaims the endlessness of His power and strength; and there is absolutely no way to overstate this. He created ALL men and women equal in His image, which is also extremely important to understand.

The Bible clearly states that, "All have sinned and fall short of the glory of God." (Romans 3:23). The Bible does not say some have sinned or most have sinned or only you have sinned. It says all humans, except for God's son, Jesus Christ, have sinned. *All* includes me, you, your parents, your children, your spouse, your teachers, and your pastor. We have all been separated from God by our sin, but thankfully we have all been given the ability to bridge that separation.

I say all of this not to judge or condemn; we get enough of that from Satan and his demons and from the world around us. I say this to let you, the reader, know that we are all on the same playing field. We are all created equal, no matter what we look like, how we speak, how much money we have, what car we drive, or especially what you have done in your past.

God created each one of us uniquely and in His perfect image, and He loves each one of us unconditionally and without boundaries. God's concept is important to understand because so often, we allow our mistakes to isolate us. We allow ourselves to feel ostracized because of our past. Or we believe that our crimes are too great to overcome and be forgiven. These are all lies that stand in the way of our future and our ability to accomplish something greater that is intended for us.

Yes, we have all screwed up. We have all done things we are not proud of or hurt someone we love. We have all said or done things that seem and feel unforgiveable. Maybe we have cheated on a spouse or stolen something from work or committed a crime. Conversely, we have all been hurt by others. We have been on the receiving end of someone else's sin or malicious act and it hurts; it hurts badly. For them, for us, for all parties involved, it hurts. All these acts create huge amounts of unforgiveness, towards God, towards others, and especially towards ourselves. Satan uses all of this to cause each and every one of us unforgiveness, sickness, anger, guilt, bitterness, resentment, and a whole slew of other negative emotions. He uses all of these, especially, unforgiveness, to hold us back from acting in accordance with God's plan for our lives.

I, just like you, was the poster child for mistakes and a sounding board for the enemy. I have screwed up. Big time! I have been given another chance, or two, or a thousand, and squandered those chances every time. God had saved me from inconceivable harm and near-death circumstances, and when the dust settled, I had gone right back to consuming drugs, drinking, gambling, and all of the other things that got me into trouble in the first place. And what was my response to narrowly escaping harm or punishment? Well, generally I would pat myself on the back and tell myself how lucky I was to have gotten out of whatever mess I had gotten myself into, never once giving God the recognition for saving me or recognizing that I needed to make massive changes to the way I was living my life.

I love history and I love reading about the Israelites in the Old Testament of the Bible and how they continually were given second chances by God and yet would always somehow fall back into the same bad habits and sinful behaviors. When I first started reading these stories years ago, I always wondered how the Israelites could keep messing up the opportunities, miracles, and second chances God was providing them. How many times do you have to lose a hundred thousand men in battle to wake up and realize you are not doing what God wants you to do? I always wondered why God included these stories in the Bible and what, if any, relevance they have to my life and the world today. Then it hit me, we are all just like the Israelites. No, most of us do not have a golden statue of a calf sitting around our house that we worship. But our "golden calf" can be anything. Anything that we put on a pedestal and give more time and energy to than God and our relationship with Him. It might be our job, or our spouse, or our kids, or money, or health, or working out or sports. And all of us, just like the Israelites, are given chance after chance to change our lives when we screw up. We are given repeated opportunities to make wholesale changes that will help reshape our future and the future of those we love. And yet again, we find ourselves making the same mistake or even different ones, and God must pick us up from the pit of despair, dust us off and tell us He loves us very much. And what do we do? Just like the Israelites we go back to our old ways or we find other ways to sin.

This continual cycle and God's unfailing response and perseverance speaks to the forgiveness, unconditional love, mercy, grace, and patience that God has for us. For most of us, recognizing these attributes of God takes a major life event or a series of events to wake us up. It could be the loss of a loved one or divorce or financial hardship that seems never ending. Or it could be the actions of your children, either young or old, that make you realize that they are following in your footsteps toward self-destruction.

In my case, the final, of many wake-up calls was the birth of my twin son and daughter, Michael and Mykala. They were born July 4, 2010, and for what happened after their birth, I will be eternally grateful to God for the rest of my days. He saved me, again, for the last time. He used their birth to shake me and wake me up to His plans for my life. He started washing away the old selfish Marcus and started filling me with His love. I love their smiles and their innocence. I am in awe of their amazing comprehension of God's love for them and all mankind. They are not scarred or broken like adults and sadly some other children. They understand the purity of God's love. In them, I have a second chance to heal old wounds and to reach those who have made a mess of their lives just like I did.

CHAPTER 2

First, I Need to Take Ownership for My Actions

꩜

The mistakes I have made are 110% my fault. I own them! No matter how I was raised or how uncomfortable my home life seemed, neither influenced the choices I made. We are all born with free will and are solely responsible for our own actions.

It is important to understand the concept of free will because once we understand that we have all been given free will to make choices with our lives, we should also be able to understand that we have to take ownership for those choices. The free will that each of us has was given to us by God in the very beginning. Genesis 2:16-17 states,

---

"and the Lord God commanded the man, "You are free to eat from any tree in the garden; but you must not eat from the tree of the knowledge of good and evil, for when you eat from it you will certainly die."

The verse talks about how Adam and Eve were given the free will to choose between obedience and sin at the beginning of mankind. This free will has been handed down to each one of us. Neither God or anyone else makes or forces us to make the choices we make. Each one of us is responsible for our own actions. From Proverbs 16:9 we read,

> "In their hearts humans plan their course, but the Lord establishes their steps."

God is the author of our lives. He knows every decision that we will make, but we still have to make those decisions. We are torn between choosing with our flesh and choosing with the Spirit of the Lord and no matter which way we choose, we have to take ownership for our actions.

Until I began writing this book, I had not fully taken responsibility for my mistakes and choices. There was still a part of me that blamed my parents. There was also a large part of me that blamed God. When I first wrote this, I caught myself thinking that if my parents had not been so hard on me or unloving towards me, then I would not have made such a mess of my life. I pondered whether I would have turned out differently? I did what I had always done, which was blame everyone else except myself for my mistakes. I was not taking ownership for my actions or the choices that I had made. I blamed how I had turned out on the environment in which I was raised. I tried to blame my mistakes on my dad because I felt like he had not loved me and was not there for me. I somehow tried to make the connection between my dad not throwing the football or baseball with me when I was a kid to me doing drugs and being arrested. I did not understand that the choices I had made were done through my own free will and not by others.

I love my parents very much and am extremely grateful for their love and sacrifices. As a family, we have learned from our past and moved on with our lives. How my parents raised me is simply a reflection of how they were raised.

My parents had me at a young age and simply did what they knew. They did the best they could based on their upbringing. The presence of God in our home and my life, although a very flawed view of Him at times, eventually saved me and many times kept me from prison and even death. I was raised like so many other churchgoing, God fearing, Christians in that God represented fear and punishment. I viewed God as standing next to me ready to smack me on the hand if I dared to cross the line between right and wrong. From what I was taught, He was comprised of rules and legalism, not unconditional love, mercy, and patience.

A couple years into this project, I finally had a version that I felt was ready for my family and others to read. The first version of this book was completely different from the one you are currently reading. After I had finished writing the first version, I was eager to let my family and a few others read it to get their feedback. Truthfully, I was proud of what *I* had accomplished. I knew that I had created a masterpiece and couldn't wait to have others confirm my great accomplishment. I shared it with my wife, Michelle, my parents, my sister, and a few others. Michelle's reaction was what I expected. She had walked beside me through this journey, so she remembers it almost exactly as I did. The ups, the downs, the pain, and the struggles. She had a front row seat to all of it. Much to my surprise and dismay, though, the response I received from everyone else was not as glowing as I had expected. My dad, mom, and sister appreciated the book and the effort I had made to put my story into writing, but they were hurt by some of what they read as the story still contained a tone of anger and unforgiveness towards them. I had also let the pastor that had originally encouraged me to write my story and go through the steps to have it published and share it with others read the first version of my book. His comments were critical and stung deeply. He did not pat me on the back and congratulate me like I wanted him to; he did just the opposite. He was very honest in pointing out that the book was filled with anger and unforgiveness from me towards my family, especially my dad. He told me that I had not taken ownership of my mistakes and my past and that my story conveyed a lack of responsibility and blame directed towards my dad. He did not feel that my story resembled a story of love and hope, but a story of bitterness and hostility.

I was stunned and upset. My initial reaction was that he obviously did not know what he was talking about. I even remember thinking that clearly, he was an angry legalistic father who couldn't come to grips with his own mistakes as a parent. My pride took control of my thoughts and clouded my perception. At the same time, part of me wondered if what he said was true, so I prayed about it. Unfortunately, I did not pray from a spirit of humility but, rather from a spirit of pride, so the answer always came back that he was obviously wrong and I could no longer value his opinion. I completely shut down on the project. If this was the response I would receive, then I did not want to share my story. I was not humble or being led by the Spirit of God, but by my own pride and unforgiveness.

But God was not done with me or my story. He was not going to quit on me even though I was willing to. I wrestled with the pastor's comments for months. I started going back and forth. One moment I was filled with anger and pride, but the next moment I was filled with a sense of remorse and shame. The more I wrestled with this the more my heart started to soften. I started praying for wisdom not from a place of pride and bitterness, but from a place of humility and repentance. I started to read my story over again and started seeing the anger and resentment in my words that others had so clearly seen. As I did this, it became apparent that I was still harboring anger and unforgiveness towards my family and God. I realized my heart was still full of unforgiveness and animosity. The pastor who gave me that feedback was absolutely correct and I was absolutely wrong. I am grateful that I allowed him to read it and that he had the courage to tell me exactly what he had read and what I needed to hear. I could finally see that my way of thinking was toxic and destructive and needed to be reconciled for me to move on from my past. I finally realized that the only way I could do this was to fully accept responsibility for my mistakes and openly give and receive forgiveness. And that is what I did.

After many years of wrestling with the creation of this book and what God's plan was for it, I realized it was God's will and my desire to save just one life. What I did not realize was that the first life it was going to save was my own. My life, my heart, and my soul were still filled with so much pain and unforgiveness and God wanted to use this process to cleanse me of that, and it did. He wanted me to relive my journey repeatedly in order to finally break through all my unforgiveness and insecurity and the pain and bitterness from my past that still held a piece of me. He wanted me to let go of the pride that I held on to so tightly and allow myself to be humbled before Him and others. God knew that the only way that I could share with others to openly give and receive unconditional love and forgiveness is if I was able to completely do the same in my own life. I could not write and tell others to forgive and be free of the past if I have not done that myself.

As I mentioned, my parents' and sister's reaction were also not what I expected. They were caught off guard by my story and my account of my childhood and young adulthood. They did not understand or realize the pain that I had felt or suffered. They had a totally different view of what had happened from what Michelle and I did. They were hurt by some of what I had written, and they were also ashamed of how they had treated us and handled the situation. This was not my intention to hurt them or rub salt in a wound. But God knew that they too had not fully been freed of their anger and unforgiveness from our past. They too had not taken responsibility for how they had treated Michelle and me and the mistakes that they had made along the way.

None of my family nor I realized this, but we needed this. We were all still carrying around wounds that had never properly healed. Forgiveness had never been completely asked for or received by any of us. My story in its early stages, although a very painful reminder of the past, was exactly what we all needed.

As I stated previously, there was still a lot of bitterness and unforgiveness in me that came out in my writing. But as much as Satan wanted to use this to harm and divide us, God had a different plan for it. God's plan was for this to cleanse and heal us. And that is what it did. There were many tears and much forgiveness given and received. Now, my story had not just helped to heal and save me, but it had done the same for my family.

Ultimately, my story and my family's is one of great pain that led to forgiveness and hope; forgiveness for the pain and hurt that we caused each other and then moving on from that and using it to better ourselves and those around us. I want others to see the hope that was created and to know that life can get better. I want those who feel alone, and even those who do not, to know that they are not alone. My story is about finding hope that when forgiveness is given and received, you can be fully cleansed. Forgiveness absolutely does this for you and everyone around you. My hope is for you, the reader, to understand that no matter how bad your circumstances may seem in life or no matter what you do or have done, you can and will always be forgiven and can change your life even when all seems lost. I know. I have been down that road before.

CHAPTER 3

Where My Journey Began

～

With all that said, here is a great place to begin.

I was born in Indiana in August 1974 to very prototypical Midwestern parents. They were married at a very young age and I came along a few years later. Both of my parents came from hard working middle to lower class families, mainly farmers and factory workers. They were raised in church-going homes, but a relationship with God was not the focal point of their upbringing. My dad graduated from bible college and went into the ministry. My mom worked various jobs while taking care of our home and family. My only sibling, a sister, was born three years after me. Dad worked hard to take care of his young family. He worked as a youth pastor at our church and other part time jobs. We did not have a lot, but we also were not aware of that either. Both of my parents worked extremely hard to provide for us. This was who they were.

We moved to Florida permanently when I was seven. My dad took a job as a youth pastor at a church and also started working for my grandparents in the family business. Our family was very active in the church and this was a big part of my early life. When I was approximately ten, my dad permanently gave up the ministry and started working full time in my grandparents' business.

From a spiritual standpoint, our home was an extremely legalistic Christian home. My parents raised me a lot like they were raised. Even though my dad was in the ministry, God, or more specifically God's grace and love and a relationship with Him, were rarely a part of our everyday lives. My upbringing felt a lot like a sandbox with a line drawn down the middle. One side represented what was right and the other side wrong. If I stayed on the right side of the sand box, all was well, but if I crossed that line, even unintentionally, punishment, specifically from my dad, seemed swift and severe at times.

I was not a bad kid. As a matter of fact, I was a pretty good kid, or so I thought. I went to a private Christian school through the eighth grade. I followed every rule at home and at school to the tee. I could recite endless amounts of Bible verses. I was a bright kid and did well in school. I was also very active and played just about every sport I could. In the sixth grade, I was asked to preach during our weekly chapel to the entire sixth through twelfth grade class at my school. My message was centered around Matthew 13, sowing your seed on the good soil. I dressed in farmer overalls and had pockets full of seeds. As I recounted the parable of sowing seeds on the different soils, I walked across the stage sowing seeds this way and that. The message was a hit.

Now, over 30 years later, as I reflect on the message I gave, I am just starting to see the validity of this parable to my journey.

I preached a few more times during middle school and always felt like I had a heart to go into the ministry, even at that age. I did not understand God or what He represented, but I knew how to follow his rules, and I knew how to share that with others. Sadly though, I had an unhealthy fear of God and my parents, which is what temporarily kept me in line. I had no real exposure to or understanding of God's love and grace. I did not even know that God's love existed or that forgiveness was an option.

Unfortunately, my fear of God, His punishment, a lack of true understanding of His love and grace, and the legalistic culture in our home induced an immeasurable amount of rebellion; a rebellion that would later cause a huge divide in my relationship with my parents. During this time, my parents both worked long hours to support our family. Working and paying bills always came before time as a family. I have very few memories of truly happy times with my family. My parents, especially my dad, were just never around or a part of my life. I played many different sports and my parents never came to watch me. My parents and God felt very absent in my life and many times I felt extremely alone.

My freshman year of high school, I transferred from the small Christian school to a large public school. This marked the beginning of the end. Before going to high school, I seemed like a confident and outgoing boy. Underneath, however, I was shy, naïve, insecure, and vulnerable. At the small private Christian school, I had lots of friends and no problem in social settings. When taken out of that element and placed into a public school where the rules of engagement were completely different from what I knew, my world was turned upside down. This rocked me to the core and a series of events my first year created massive amounts of insecurity and self-esteem issues that I have spent a lifetime trying to heal.

When I look back now, I realize this is when I truly started to feel isolated. My family had switched churches at this time, and I had changed to a new school. All the friends I had were gone in a matter of a few months. Also, my parents worked long hours, which made this feeling of loneliness worse. So, I was alone when I rode the bus to and from school. I was alone at school. And I was alone at home.

That first year of high school was really a struggle. I was the guy sitting by himself every day in the lunchroom. It was tough! Because of my birthday and my parents starting me in school at age four, I was always about a year younger than the other kids in my grade, so when everyone else had hit puberty, I was still a full year behind. Also, I was always the smallest kid in my class in school.

Genetics were not doing me any favors. In eighth grade, my sister who was three years younger, was about a foot taller than me. Or at least it felt that way. All of this created and led to more and more insecurity in me. When I look back at pictures of me when I started high school, I looked like I should have been in the fourth grade.

My first few months of high school, I was teased and made fun of constantly. So, the only way I knew how to cope was to hide. Many times, I would leave class for no reason and go sit in the bathroom by myself. I did not talk to other kids and I did not interact with other kids. I figured not being noticed was the best way to protect myself against being made fun of. My sophomore year was not much better, but at least I finally hit puberty and started to catch up in size to other kids. So, the first couple of years of high school, it felt like I walked the halls of school alone. Almost all the friends I had were from my church, so this was the only place I truly felt like I fit in. But I was only at church for a few hours a week. I was so handcuffed by fear and insecurity that I did not know how to interact with others. The only real memories I have from this time in my life was being on my own. Many times, I wondered and questioned, "Where is God if He even exists? Why me? Would this ever end?"

As I became acclimated to public school, I slowly began to realize that the world I had lived in for fourteen years was not a true reflection of what the world around me was. I was exposed to things that I did not know existed up until that point. I started listening to music and watching movies that I had never been allowed to watch. The kids at my new school talked and said things that I had never heard. Everyone dressed and acted differently from the kids at the small private school I had attended previously. I knew kids from my church that went to my school, but no one ever talked about God. My parents had done such a good job of sheltering me from the world around us that I was truly naïve to what the real world was like. I was overwhelmed and terrified by much of this, but it also created a sense of excitement in me as I became more and more exposed to it.

At the same time, as I was dealing with the changes at school and in my social life, my home life started to deteriorate rapidly. My dad, unfortunately, became extremely ill. He could barely get out of bed. Over the course of a few months, he could no longer work. He was miserable and frail; he had no idea what was causing his suffering. His illness negatively impacted our family interaction. He was raised in a home with parents who emphasized the value of hard work. His work and work ethic partly defined his existence and purpose. My dad's mystery illness was slowly beginning to deteriorate his perception. This mystery illness was taking all of this away from him. Because he could not work, my parents' financial burden grew exponentially. He became angry, frustrated, and confused with his circumstances. Of course, this overflowed into our relationship, which prompted even more questions about God. Why was this happening to my dad? Why was this happening to us? Where was God?

The combination of school life and home life became a toxic mix. As I started to pull away from my parents and started doing things that were on the other side of the line in the sandbox, my parents tried to exert more and more control over me. It felt like their response to most of my actions was filled with judgment and anger. The only time I felt like I saw God was when we went to church every Sunday and Wednesday night or when I did something that my parents felt was wrong. To me, God represented rules and guidelines, and when those were not followed explicitly, God represented anger and punishment. I truly believe that my parents felt like they were losing control of me, so their solution was to exert more control on me than they already were. They tried to control what I listened to, what I watched, and who I hung out with, which are things that all parents should be actively a part of in their children's lives. But for me, the line that I was not allowed to cross on many of these things felt overbearing and extreme.

I remember sometime around the age of fourteen I had gone to the mall with my best friend from church. He listened to music that I knew I would never be allowed to listen to: Beastie Boys, Bon Jovi, Kid and Play—classic 80's music. I had never listened to music like this before. We went to the mall to the music store to buy some new tapes. I had always loved the music from the 60's and 70's. I remember listening to *Bread* albums with my dad in the garage a few times when he was working on something as a kid. I picked out a *Beatles* tape. I was so happy. I thought my parents would love it. It was from their generation, so why wouldn't they? I took it home and played it for my parents. Their reaction was not at all what I expected. They became upset with me for buying this tape and said it was ungodly. They were angry and judgmental. I did not understand why they reacted that way and they did not take the time to explain to me why I should not listen to that music. They simply said it was bad and destructive and they were upset with me. I remember being very confused by their reaction. This type of response was common in my relationship with my parents and this created and triggered animosity and rebellion.

Unfortunately, the more my parents pushed, the more I pushed back. In looking back, I realize it was at this point in my life that my view of my Heavenly Father and that of my earthly father started to mirror each other. I felt judged, unloved, and forgotten by both, which left me feeling empty and bitter internally and towards them.

CHAPTER 4

Turning My Back on Dad and God

꿍

As the distance grew between my family and me, especially with my dad, it also grew in my relationship with God. I distanced myself farther and farther away from my parents and God. I felt so alone at this time and my dad never spent time with me. God felt very much the same way. I could not see or hear God. I did not even know how to. God, just like my dad, was very absent in my day to day life. In my mind, both my dad and God were one in the same. Neither felt like they were around and neither seemed like they wanted to have anything to do with me, so I turned my back on them. I figured they would not even notice I was gone. I did not know what a father's love looked like from my earthly father, so I certainly did not know that it was possible for my Heavenly Father to love me.

Unfortunately, my dad's sickness worsened, and he was still unable to work. At the same time, my parents had closed on building a home prior to my Dad getting ill, and they were forced to move forward with its construction. My mom was then forced to be the sole source of income for our family, which increased the financial burden on my parents creating compounding pressure on them to keep our family afloat. This pressure was evident in our day to day lives. My dad was virtually bed-ridden for several months and not getting better. He became more and more exhausted and frustrated with his health and his inability to provide for us. I remember my dad being frustrated and angry at my mom and me quite often. I constantly felt like I was walking on eggshells. Nothing I did felt like it was right. I guess I had finally gotten my dad's attention. Unfortunately, it consisted primarily of anger and frustration. The burden on my parents, especially my dad, was too much for him and us to bear.

To make matters worse for him and us, no Western or mainstream doctor could tell him what was physically wrong with him. This mystery illness was destroying everything in my dad's life; his finances, his ability to work, and most importantly, his relationship with his family. What was later discovered by a natural health doctor who was new to our area, Dr. Jim Hogsed, was that my dad had Chronic Fatigue Syndrome. Dr. Jim's son had battled with Chronic Fatigue Syndrome, so he was able to identify and help treat my dad when many other doctors could not. Little was known about Chronic Fatigue Syndrome twenty-five years ago, but thankfully it was treatable and my dad was able to start down the slow road to recovery. Unfortunately, the damage to our family and our relationship had been done. There was no going back.

All the hopelessness and insecurity I was dealing with at school, along with the anger, confusion, and feeling unloved at home became too much for me. My memories of this time in life are only of feeling alone and unwanted. Life truly felt hopeless and meaningless. I felt like my dad and God had walked away from me for good. Content in my conclusion, I turned my back on my dad and God. In my mind, they were not there for me anyways, so I was simply doing what had already been done to me. I no longer wanted or felt like I needed either of them as a part of my life.

I started drinking during this time and completely distanced myself from my family, God, and school. I was forced to go to church and got nothing out of it. I was so turned off to God that the words being spoken by my pastor, youth pastor, and parents were hollow and empty and represented nothing more than oppression. I still wasn't a bad kid and I still had a moral compass that had been instilled in me from how I had been raised, but I was starting to have fun and all the things my parents were telling me not to do were more exciting than the things they were telling me to do. I was now a senior in high school, content with my decision to live my life as I intended and not what God, or my parents had intended.

And then my life really changed course. At the start of my senior year in high school, I met my first real girlfriend and now wife, twenty-nine plus years later, Michelle. She was beautiful then, and she is even more beautiful now. How I managed to get a girl like her to stay with me for more than a week, let alone twenty-nine years, is a mystery that only God knows.

Michelle and I have experienced challenges and triumphs. We have been through a lot, and I put her through a lot. I am eternally grateful to her for sticking with me and always seeing the good in me when no one else, including myself, saw it. She was not raised in a Christian home, and this fact served as another wedge in my family life. My parents and sister verbally disapproved of my relationship with her because she was not a Christian. Their disapproval led to many arguments. As my family continued to disapprove of my relationship with Michelle, like everything else they disapproved of, I gravitated more and more towards her. Looking back, she really was my only lifeline out of an extremely unhappy and unhealthy home life. I had no one else to turn to, and the people who should have showed me unconditional love, mercy, and grace were the ones pushing me farther away. My family simply shut down on me because they did not approve of my life or Michelle.

An example of this came in the fall of 1991, my senior year. I had been dating Michelle for a few months and went to her house to watch a football game with friends. Like most weekends, I used this as an opportunity to drink and party. After the game, I drove home. As I pulled into the garage in my parent's Thunderbird, I pulled in a little too far. Thankfully, I did not drive through the wall. Unfortunately, though against the front wall of the garage was a floor fan and I did manage to drive into it. This made a loud crunching noise that no parent could miss, especially my parents who happened to be right inside the garage door at that exact moment. They were mad when they came out of the door, and they were furious when they smelled alcohol on my breath.

What happened next was trivial and inconsequential as an adult looking back, but it really changed my view of God well into my adulthood. We went inside, and my parents began reading scripture to me and weeping over me and praying for me. The focus was about God's disappointment with me and how my actions were leading me to hell. I was being fed a message of guilt and condemnation. I am not sure how long this went on for, but I was numb to all of it. The most vivid part of this story for me was waking up the next morning and realizing that I was not really in hell as they had professed. I had not been consumed by a giant ball of fire. Actually, I was relatively unscathed. Sure, my parents were upset and disappointed with me, but that felt normal. My parents had spent much time and energy the day before telling me that my choices were going to send me to hell, but since I had not woken up in an eternal fiery pit, as I was led to believe by them, everything they and God were telling me about my life and the choices I was making was wrong.

My behavior did not change the last few years of high school or first two years of college. Michelle was two years behind me in school, so I attended the local state college in order to be close to her. Living at home and my relationship with my family was a blur. I had a job and I worked hard at it. Between school and work, I did not have a lot of free time. The free time I did have, I spent with Michelle and I was usually intoxicated. As Michelle was getting closer to her high school graduation, she made the decision to attend the University of South Florida in Tampa. So, of course, I decided to go there also. It was two hours away, so it was close to home, but also far enough away that I could begin to live my own life.

Finally, I would be free to live my life the way I desired when I moved out of my parents' house. Free to make my own decisions and follow my own set of rules. I would finally be free of the anger and arguing and judgment of my parents and God.

But the question that would soon be answered is would I be mature enough to handle this freedom and make wise decisions with my life? Could I handle all this newfound freedom and the responsibility that came with it?

The LOVE *of a* FATHER

CHAPTER 5

When I Finally Felt Free

～

It is the summer of 1994 and I had a few weeks before I was moving to Tampa to attend USF. I was getting ready to finally be on my own. It felt like the start of a whole new life for me. I was excited and ready to move on and start a new adventure free of my parents and God. Life felt like it was pretty good.

And then the inconceivable happened!

I got arrested for the first time.

My parents and sister had gone on vacation, so I was home alone. The night before they got home, I went out and got really drunk. On my way home, I was stopped at a stoplight and don't ask what set me off, probably the combination of a lot of beer and my teenage boy testosterone, but I got extremely angry at a car next to me filled with five high school aged kids. When the light went green, I went crazy. I chased after them and tried to run them off the road. Earlier that week, I had bought a pellet gun that looked just like a real gun, so I decided to pull it out and wave it at them. Smart move! They made a series of turns and I followed them. The last turn they made happened to be down the same road that a county sheriff car was on coming from the other direction. They stopped him and screamed that they were being chased by some lunatic who was waving a gun at them. There was nowhere for me to go.

I pulled over, and within what felt like seconds, I had about six real guns pointed in my face. They pulled me out of the car and searched it. They found the pellet gun, much to my humiliation, and laughed. The irony is, I was generally non-confrontational and raised in a nonviolent home. Guns and violence were not allowed nor were they accepted by my family. Yet, here I was a stupid kid waiving a pellet gun around. The cops were really amused by all of this, for which I do not blame them. I was not a hardened criminal; just a kid with little to no common sense making really stupid decisions. They arrested me on a misdemeanor carrying a concealed weapon charge, and for that, I got to spend the night in jail. My grandma bailed me out the next morning.

That day, I sat alone in my house asking myself the same questions over and over again. How could I be so stupid? What was I doing with my life? How had I gotten to this point? And the most frightening of all—what were my parents going to say? They were returning from vacation that day, and I needed to figure out what, if any, defense or reasonable explanation I could conjure. When they finally arrived, the only way I can put it is it did not go well. I was so overwhelmed with tons of emotions, like fear and anxiety, that I had to tell them right away. I knew that this was not something I could or should hide from them. Also, a huge part of me was afraid of what was going to happen to me and what the consequences for my mistake would be. I needed and wanted my family to console and tell me it was going to be ok. I just wanted to get it over with. My parents had not even pulled in the driveway and started unpacking the car and I laid it on them. Wow, they were angry! I had seen my dad get mad at me plenty of times before this, but this was a whole new level of anger. My mom was mad at me. Even my sister was mad at me. And so, the battle began.

There was a lot of yelling and anger and tears; a lot of questions from them towards me and towards themselves. They were asking me questions like, "how could I have done something so stupid?"

and "what was I thinking?" As any parent knows, I was clearly not thinking. I am sure they were trying to figure out how we had gotten to this point and were partially blaming themselves for this mess. I had screwed up big time. Unlike other times when I had been caught doing something wrong, this time, I promised my parents that changes would be made and that I would "turn to God." They believed me, and to my surprise, did not exact punishment on me. For the next two weeks before I left for school in Tampa, I was a model citizen. Although I said and did the right things for those two weeks, what did "turn my life over to God" really mean?

Honestly, I had no idea. I think both my family and I just expected I would know how to repent, but I had never seen what it meant to repent or what a true relationship with Jesus Christ looked like. I did not even know that having a relationship with Jesus was possible. My parents had never shown me how to truly get on my knees and lay my sins at the foot of the cross and ask for forgiveness. Other than praying before we ate and at bedtime, I did not know what true prayer looked like. I had not been shown how to open up to God and ask him to walk beside me and guide me. I was not aware that I should have asked the Holy Spirit to fill me with his presence and to guide me into better choices for my life and to convict me when my choices were not following God's commands. I had never seen my parents do any of these things so I did not know where to start. I also think my parents were in shock, so they did not know what to do. And I think most other people around us were still stuck in the fire and brimstone mode, so their response was one of condemnation and judgment instead of support. No one stepped in to guide me towards God; not my family or a pastor—no one. Again, I was alone without guidance on how to really make the wholesale changes that needed to be made. I had no real-life example to follow on how to turn my life to God, so I did not even know where to start.

Months after my arrest, consequentially, I was sentenced to a fine and the charges were expunged from my permanent record; a slap on the wrist with no significant consequences. My journey into my newfound freedom was not off to the best of starts. This was not the beginning I had planned to my big adventure. As I reflected on the incident over my last couple of weeks before leaving for Tampa, I just believed it was one stupid mistake that I would never make again. Besides, I was not going to let one little mistake overshadow the next chapter in my life. It was time for the prodigal son to shake it off and move on. I told myself, no more stupid mistakes. Apparently, I did not listen very well.

The day finally came when I moved to Tampa to attend USF. It was awesome! It was a big school in a big city with lots to do and see and most importantly, I was finally free. I absolutely love the movie *The Shawshank Redemption* probably because I can relate to so much of the movie. One of my favorite parts is when Andy, played by Tim Robbins, finally escapes by crawling a half mile down a sewage drain and is standing in the creek in the pouring rain and raises his hands in the air as if to say, "FREEDOM!" This is how I felt. I viewed this as my "get out of jail free" card. In my mind, I was free of what felt like bondage and oppression from my family and God. I did not appreciate the life my parents had tried to provide, the sacrifices they had made, or the love that they had for me. I was just finally free.

College was wild and fun and crazy! Michelle and I immediately joined a sorority and fraternity, respectively, which provided instant friends and parties. My college years were like those of so many other college kids. My focus became less and less about school and more and more about partying. It felt great to finally be accepted and have friends. I partied seven days a week without ever coming up for air.

This reckless and out of control lifestyle led to a couple more brushes with the law. Twice in my first two years at USF, I got pulled over while I was intoxicated. Both times I was doing stupid things while driving that just so happened to be when a police officer was around. Both times I was fortunate and did not get a DUI. The first resulted in a misdemeanor arrest for minor in possession of alcohol, which I ended up getting another slap on the wrist for, and the second resulted in a Careless Driving ticket. And yet again, I got by relatively unscathed. I never once considered that God might have been watching out for me. I just chalked it up to blind dumb luck.

What did my family think?

Thankfully, they had no idea. I rarely talked to them, unless I went back home to Fort Myers, which usually only included holidays. And this was before cell phones, so I never called because I was too busy having fun. And of course, I would never have told them about all the partying I was doing and especially not about my brushes with the law. That would have just brought more arguing and pain into all our lives. I think our relationship was generally nonexistent, and none of us either recognized this or knew how to correct it, so we became uncomfortably content with this status.

I am not sure how I made it through this time without more instability in my life or how I even managed to get relatively good grades in school, but I did. Going to class was just an opportunity for me to finally catch up on some sleep. No offense to my professors. I also managed to hold down my job that I had held since I was eighteen. I never missed work, and when I was there, I worked very hard. But still the most important thing in my life was partying and having fun. I had no direction and no idea what I wanted to do with my life. I bounced through about six different majors before I finally settled on Accounting mainly because that was the one I was closest to achieving.

Michelle also was an Accounting major, but she was my polar opposite when it came to studying. Sure, she liked to have fun, just like me, but she also worked very hard at school. She understood how to balance her social life and her school life. She studied and worked extremely hard and because of her diligence, she achieved a lot during her under-graduate and graduate career. So, what was I doing while she was studying? You guessed it. Partying and living it up.

Unfortunately, this routine and my increasingly wild and out of control behavior started to wear on our relationship. As expected, we drifted apart. We had different plans for our lives. Mainly, she had a plan and I did not. I had put Michelle through a lot. I had gotten in trouble with the law several times and it always seemed like she was the one trying help me pick up the pieces afterwards. My actions and my erratic and out of control behavior constantly put a strain on our relationship. I never did any schoolwork or studied for tests, but as soon as it was the night before a test in a class we had together, I would panic and beg her to help me prepare. She knew without it, I would fail and Michelle never wanted me to fail or feel like a failure. So, she gave in every time. It was always a fire drill. As a matter of fact, our lives were always a fire drill because of me. She was always there to bail me out of whatever mess I got myself into and I think this was starting to take its toll on her. She was starting to reach a breaking point and I just did not see it. Michelle just wanted me to live life with some semblance of self-control. She was extremely organized and prepared for everything and I was the complete opposite. I did not even know how to do any of this. I did not know how to be in control or prepared or organized. I was a runaway train without any brakes. We argued a lot and I went out all the time without her. The more she pushed me, the more I started to push away from her. This was the same thing that had happened with my parents.

The harder they pushed, the harder I pushed away. The stability I had in Michelle was starting to crumble. The more it crumbled, the more I ran away. I was constantly flirting with and talking to other girls. I finally decided to break up with her for what ended up being the shortest break up in history, maybe two days tops. I went out with another girl I had been talking to, which might have been the shortest date in history, maybe thirty minutes. We did not even make it to where we were going and I turned the car around and dropped the girl off and immediately drove to Michelle's house.

Deep inside, I knew I did not want to lose her. We tried to fix our relationship on our own, but it was the same thing over and over again. I would do something reckless or out of control or have an emotional outburst and things would escalate. An argument would always ensue. Once the dust settled, we would sit and try to talk things out. I would inevitably promise to change and not do whatever I had done to start the argument again. I always promised changes. But this never helped because we were both still immature emotionally and spiritually. God was not present in either of our lives at this point. I went to church only when I was home with my family, which was maybe a few weekends a year. I had completely pushed God out of my life and I felt like I was firmly in control. It was a rocky period in our relationship, but we did somehow manage to stay together. We were both searching for the answer to what would fix our relationship and us.

And then, out of nowhere, it hit me. Finally, I found what I believed would solve all our relationship and communication problems. I believed I had found what would fix our "love" and what would bring us back together. This one thing was the answer to all of the arguing, anger, and distance that had grown between us. This was it. The solution seemed so easy and innocent.

The LOVE *of a* FATHER

CHAPTER 6

The Beginning of The End

❧

A nd this is where the real story begins.

Now, in retrospect, I can see clearly just how big of a mess every aspect of my life was. I drank in excess every day of the week. I never took a night off. I had had several run ins with the law and I am not sure how I had not killed myself or someone else. It was also a wonder to my friends and those around me how something more tragic had not happened. Everyone around me saw my reckless behavior except me. I had virtually no relationship with my parents or God. I never spoke to them and, honestly, I just did not care. If they had been a greater part of my life, they would have just been disappointed and disapproved, which would have led to more conflict than was already present.

I was a mess in school. I barely went to class and when I did, I was normally pretty hungover. I am not sure how I continued to get good grades, but I did. I had started and stopped several different majors in college and always grew restless with the one I was currently engaged in. A large part of this was I did not want to graduate and have to migrate from a crazy partying college student to an adult with a job and responsibilities. Ugh, responsibility! This did not sound fun and really felt like it was going to kill my social life. Also, and more significantly, I was afraid of the unknown. I was truly a ship without a rudder sailing through the night. I had absolutely no direction in my life and this terrified me. I had no idea what I wanted to do with my life and bouncing from one major to another just put off the decision that I knew I would eventually have to make. Everyone around me seemed so focused and sure of their path. Michelle never wavered with her path and this just made me feel more out of place and unsure of myself. Insecurity had a firm grip on every aspect of my life. Worst of all, my and Michelle's relationship was also a train-wreck. How and why did she stay with me? I was completely emotionally unstable. I was constantly racing out of control and this behavior spilled over into our relationship. We were constantly arguing and then trying to make up, but this strategy was just putting a band-aid on it and I was constantly ripping the band-aid off. I was dragging her and us deeper and deeper into a pit of despair and anxiety. I knew she was frustrated with me and us. Michelle was just trying to survive. I did not realize it, but I was also truly frustrated with myself and what I had become.

My only answer to all of the problems and the stress from my daily life was partying and alcohol. It was the only answer I could ever come up with that felt like it made all of the pain go away. The more my problems and stress had grown over the years, the harder I drank and partied. This behavior had started in high school and had just continued to get worse and worse as I was in college. I did not know how you could party or drink any more, but every day seemed like a new day and opportunity to try. I just tried to bury all of my problems in alcohol. My whole life had been about living in extremes, so drinking constantly in excess was the only way I knew how to dull the pain and make everything around me go away. I buried myself and hid in alcohol. It was my out. It was my answer to everything. It was the only way I felt like I could solve my and Michelle's relationship problems. But it **never** worked. It only made things worse. My life just continually spiraled out of control. I just never saw this. I never saw the damage that alcohol was doing to my life and the lives of those around me. So, I continued to push harder and harder. I started searching for other answers to our problems. I searched for other ways to help make the pain and struggle in my life feel normal or disappear. And that's when it happened. That's when I found what I thought would be the answer. I finally discovered what would make our relationship whole again and something that would mask the pain even better than alcohol.

The answer, or so I thought, was ecstasy. No, I do not mean being really, really happy. This story would be pretty dull and a lot less painful if it was. I mean ecstasy—the drug.

Now, I know what all of you are thinking. *Under what circumstances could that ever be the answer to relationship problems?* Trust me; it was not, and it is not. At the time, however, it seemed so harmless. It felt like this was the band aid that our relationship needed. In hindsight, it was just the opposite.

I had never taken drugs, and ironically, I looked down on friends who I knew who smoked weed. Never in a million years would I have even considered taking drugs. Drinking was one thing, but taking drugs felt way over the line. Yet, I found myself considering its benefits, at a minimum, for my relationship.

At the same time, I had a roommate who started partying with his work friends taking ecstasy. I did not know he was doing it, but I did notice a change in his behavior. I found out through a mutual friend and was shocked, but at the same time, I was curious about what ecstasy was and how it made people feel. When I asked my roommate, he made it sound so simple and harmless and even said it is no different from drinking. He explained that ecstasy made you love everything and everybody: it was also used by counselors to help mental patients and to heal relationship issues. And there you have it. It makes you loving towards others, can heal relationship issues, and is no different from drinking. These were the words I thought I needed to hear. This is what could heal my and Michelle's relationship. It seemed so easy.

The hardest part was going to be getting Michelle to go along with this plan. It took a lot of coercing and manipulation, but Michelle reluctantly agreed to this. I know she knew this was not the answer, but I also think she was desperate to try anything and did it to appease me. She wanted to save our relationship so badly that she was even willing to try something she knew was wrong in order to fix it.

Taking ecstasy for the first time was terrifying. I had never done anything like this. There was a tremendous amount of fear and terror coursing through my body. My conscious and my subconscious were screaming at me, "DON'T DO THIS!" But that voice sounded like God and my dad to me. And of course, I was not going to listen to them. Actually, this made it even more exciting. It was like the forbidden fruit that I knew I should not eat but something told me that this would open my eyes to a whole new way of thinking and living. And it did.

This was the beginning of the end.

Taking drugs changed me. No, not right away, but slowly. If you do or do not know anything about ecstasy, especially the kind I took 20 years ago, you do not take it every day, generally. You do not really become addicted to it the same way you would prescription meds, heroin, or cocaine. It was more of a party drug that you took on the weekends; just like drinking. At the end of the weekend, you can stop and resume your normal life and then repeat the next weekend. This became my new normal.

It felt as innocent as drinking, and surprisingly, it did kind of put a band aid on my and Michelle's relationship. I continued this routine weekly. I partied hard on the weekend and then tried to focus on school and work the rest of the week. Eventually, my use of ecstasy led to taking other drugs.

I started taking steroids. I loved working out and steroids seemed to make this even better. This seemed like the answer to all the self-esteem issues and unhappiness with my physical appearance that I had dealt with since my first year in high school. I tried a few other types of drugs, but nothing really stuck until I tried GHB. This quickly became my new favorite drug. To me, it was way better then drinking or anything else for that matter. It intensified the effects of whatever I was taking, whether it was ecstasy or alcohol, and it really helped me feel better when I was coming down. But GHB was dangerous and was easy to take too much. This was a bad combination for someone who lived in such extremes. My personality was all or nothing, so when I did something, I always went over the top; and GHB was no exception. Of course, this amplified my already reckless and out of control lifestyle and led to countless incidents where I could have ended up in jail or even worse— seriously injured or killed myself and/or others. My drug use continued to suck me in deeper down the path to destruction.

This pattern of behavior continued and intensified for a couple more years. Somewhere along the way, I did manage to finish my bachelor's degree in Accounting and entered the work force. I bounced around from one void less occupation to another. My weekend and sometimes mid-week routine were generally the same. We hit the clubs, strip clubs, and raves like clockwork.

I also managed to get a DUI during this time period. I was barely over the limit because I hadn't drunk that much, but I had taken so much GHB that I blacked out while driving home from a club. Unfortunately, my friend who was with me had also passed out. The terrifying thing is I honestly have no idea who was driving the car. I somehow ended up running a stop light in an area nowhere near my house, and a cop happened to be right behind me. I have no idea how I even got there, and I am eternally grateful that I did not hurt anyone on that night and the many, many other days and nights I drove in that state.

Again, I got out of this situation without too much pain and suffering. God was trying to get my attention, but I was having none of it. I was so far from God that I could not even see His hand of protection at work in my life. I never stopped to look at my life and what my decisions were doing to me and the ones around me. I was caught in a perpetual cycle of sin and recklessness and I just kept pushing harder and harder against God's voice, as the chaos of my life kept becoming greater and greater. I now know and see that God was trying to use these situations to get my attention. He was allowing me to fail in order to try to wake me up. The problem was I never saw it that way. Every time I managed to flirt with trouble and destruction and then find my way out of it, I simply gave myself all of the credit. I never saw God protecting me. In my mind, it was always me who had been the deliverer. God was trying to wake me up before I caused real damage to my life. He was trying to use these minor bumps in my path to shake me and cause change in my life. But that was never going to happen because I was so entrenched in the reckless and destructive path that I was on that I did not see any other way.

To this point, I had only used drugs and had never even considered selling them. I had a couple of close friends who I bought from and who were selling to make some extra money. I saw this and it piqued the curiosity of the entrepreneurial side of me. As a kid I loved to have lemonade sales and toy sales to my neighbors and family, so this did not seem much different. It looked so easy and the money seemed great. What could it hurt? I jumped in with both feet. I started selling drugs on a small scale, maybe 20 to 30 pills a night, while I was out. It was great because I could pay for my night and earn extra money on the side. This quickly grew for me. Each weekend, I was selling more and more and making more and more money. Through all of this, I got reconnected with an old friend who needed a source for larger quantities of ecstasy. The first time I made a sale to him, it was probably 500 pills or so. I was freaking out! This was completely different then a friend coming up to me in a club and asking for 10 pills. I was handling a lot of pills and I remember the fear and terror from that night as if it were yesterday. I even remember thinking after it was done that I would never do that again. It just felt too big! But the money was great. I made a couple grand for a couple hours work and some stress.

In the days after, once I had calmed down, it did not seem as big of a deal. All I was seeing were dollar signs, not the danger signs that were flashing in my head. I immediately started selling a larger number of pills to my new connection a couple of times a week. I did not know much about him or where the pills were going, but I did find out he was just a middleman selling to "friends" of his from up north.

The money was great and it opened a whole new world to me. My life was crazy and what I saw and did was crazy! Partying at strip clubs and clubs nearly every night of the week with my friends was awesome. Doing anything and everything was how I lived my life. Michelle and I had gotten engaged in December of 1998 and our relationship was cruising along nicely. She and I traveled to Vegas several times as we had plenty of cash and loved to party and gamble. At the time, life was a never-ending party for us. We were out of control, and yet, at the same time, things seemed so perfect!

And that is the trap that Satan wants to draw us into. Satan makes the world around look so great and seem so enticing. He lures us in by showing us how much fun we will have and how great we will feel. But Satan never shows us what it will look and feel like on the other side. He never shows us all of the damage and destruction these choices will do to our lives and the lives of those around us. He does not show us how we will look or feel the next morning when we wake up. This is what makes it so easy because we never see the consequences. I remember one of my many trips to Vegas. We had been partying for days in clubs, casinos, private mansions and strip clubs. This was my normal. One of the nights we ended up at a private party at a suite on the top floor of a famous hotel in Vegas. There were strippers, escorts, and adult film stars everywhere. It was crazy. I had been partying for days and pretty much did anything you put in front of me. I remember injecting what I was told was Special K into me from a syringe that someone just handed me. I just did not care what the consequences were. The party was out of control and I was right at home. I had been partying so hard for so many days that my body finally had had enough. I started to lose consciousness. I do not remember much after a certain point, but I do remember friends carrying me out of the hotel. The next morning, I woke up alone in my hotel room. I was completely disoriented and had no idea how I had gotten there. As I started to come to, I looked around the room and there was blood everywhere. The sheets, the wall, everything was covered in blood. There were pools of blood on the floor. I was lying face down in one when I came to. It looked like someone had been murdered. I stumbled into the bathroom and looked in the mirror and to my horror the blood had come from me. I was covered in it. This really shook me. I knew somewhere deep inside of me that I was continually flirting with death and this had been just another one of those moments. I knew that the consequences of my crazy and out of control lifestyle would catch up with me. But this never stopped me. This was Satan's trap and at that time, it worked. So much so, that even when I would wake up in a pool of my own blood after days of partying, I still only saw the pleasure and not the damage it was causing me.

As someone who now recognizes the damage and destruction I was causing myself, I still cannot falsely proclaim that living in the world and doing bad things automatically makes you feel bad and leads to hard times. It might, but it also might not. I got caught, as you will read, but I also know other people that did not, and they were able to step away from that life without losing their life or ending up in jail. So bad things do not always happen to bad people, and I, as a Christian cannot sell it this way. This is the great challenge for me personally. How do I actually communicate this to my kids and those around me without allowing legalism to oversimplify it and yet still communicate the dangers and pitfalls of the world around us in a way that is realistic and driven towards God and not away from Him? All I know is, sin and the pleasure from sin are very fleeting. It feels good for a time, but it is so very temporary. I do not care who you are or what you want to tell yourself or others, but if you live your life this way you will never be truly happy. You will never find true joy and peace.

In December of 1999, my "business" got taken to a whole new level. I was able to cut out my initial contact and got directly connected with his two buyers from up north. These two guys were ex-military and were from North Carolina. They were well connected over a large area, so they had a huge network and it was growing. They sold a little bit of everything: ecstasy, cocaine, marijuana, guns. At the same time, I ran into another old friend from college, who could handle supplying the volume of drugs that I needed to keep up with my out of state buyers. My old college friend and new supplier was also well connected with the type of people you did not want to screw over. I did not know much about him, but I did have an unhealthy dose of fear for him.

So now I was buying from and selling large amounts of drugs, mainly ecstasy, to and from guys that I did not know much about who were well connected to people who could do me great bodily harm. Little piece of advice, this is NOT a good business model. For those starting or running a business, I would not recommend using this as your blueprint for success.

So how was I getting these drugs to my buyers in North Carolina?

Well, the primary way was overnighting them via Fed Ex and UPS. I would vacuum seal 1,000 pills in a bag and send several bags in a box every couple of days. Then, a few days later, I would get a package with cash vacuum sealed in plastic bags back from them. I would get packages with $30K, $40K, maybe $50K in it at a time back from them.

Larger shipments of drugs required either me or my buyers drive the drugs back and forth. I can tell you there is a lot of fear and anxiety, as well as adrenaline, coursing through your body when you are driving a trunk full of drugs up and down the interstate for hours at a time. It feels like every car behind you is an undercover cop and is following you. In hindsight, some of them probably were. The only thing that felt like it made it worth it was the large packages of cash that I would bring back.

I had to pay for my out of control lifestyle somehow. My morning work consisted of counting the cash I was getting. I would get up and spend hours counting the money and drugs. This is when I started making serious money and things got really out of control. This routine went on for about six months until June 2000. These six months were a total blur. I am not sure how, but I was partying even harder than ever. I was starting to get connected with more and more people from different walks of life and being exposed to different opportunities that pulled me farther away from God and would have led me down an even darker path. I was traveling, partying with people I had never imagined and living a life I had never dreamed of before.

But unfortunately, there is another side to this story. The life I was living was not all fun and games. Sure, there were moments of fun, but the reality was it was all coming at a cost.

My relationship with my family was nonexistent. I had completely walked away from them and wanted nothing to do with them. Also, Michelle and I did not realize it at the time, but we were becoming more and more depressed and dependent. All the drugs and alcohol were harmfully affecting the chemical and genetic composition of our brains and our bodies. Our lives seemed so great to those around us, but really, we were just trying to make it from one weekend to the next in order to start the whole cycle over again. I was partying pretty much every night and could only go to sleep if I took enough GHB and various pills to make me pass out. We were in constant survival mode. Our lives were toxic and reckless and deep inside of us was a massive void that was getting exponentially bigger.

For every crazy story I have about partying in clubs and strip clubs and the crazy things I saw and did, there is a story about how I somehow avoided getting arrested or getting in an accident while driving when I was high and had bags, bottles, and plates of drugs in my car. Even more frightening is that I had survived near-death moments. I was constantly pushing my body harder and harder. Everything I did was in extremes. I was constantly overdosing on GHB and several times I woke up in pools of my own blood because I had cut myself or taken too much of another drug, so I was bleeding out. I do not know how or why, but miraculously these times I had passed out face down.

This is the part that is the hardest for me to communicate to the reader. I just cannot stress enough the fact that when I look back on all the things I did, none of it was worth the cost of doing it.

As I sit and think about the pain and suffering that drugs caused me then and even now, not one of the memories that I have of the partying and the life I was living was worth it. The memories fade quickly, as do your brain cells, but the pain, depression or other effects do not.

CHAPTER 7

When the Party Is Over

❧

And then my world came crashing in around me!
The party finally came to an end.
I do not remember the exact date, but sometime at the end of May 2000, I received a phone call from one of my buyers from up north. This call would change my life forever and shook me to the core. The conversation we had is a blur now, but essentially, he told me that his partner had been set up by someone and had been arrested. What I did not know at the time was he was the one who had rolled over on his partner and he was setting me up also. He was calling to let me know that the cops knew about me and that his partner was rolling over on all of us. Because the two of them were ex-military and had been networking and selling within the active military and to other ex-military, this had become a really big deal in a hurry. It was all over the news. He was freaking out! I was freaking out! I cannot even begin to recall the thoughts and fear that went through my mind, but I knew the police were coming for me. I knew that I was in way over my head and that my life was about to be turned upside down. All the money and partying and good times stopped in the blink of an eye. It was all gone and what was left was terror, fear, insecurity, and a huge void. Emptiness.

The next few days after getting this call were ones filled with terror and paranoia. I did not know what to do or to whom to turn. I certainly could not tell my parents. Our relationship had somehow managed to get worse. My dad and I were not speaking to each other. As a matter of fact, I wanted nothing to do with him, and in my mind, I thought he felt the same way.

Months earlier that year, we had a serious falling out. We were so angry with each other and so many hurtful things had been said to each other. I never wanted to speak to him again and did not want him ever to be a part of my life again. So, calling him for help was out of the question. Of course, it never even occurred to me to reach out to God. I mean, what was He going to do? I thought, God will probably just judge and condemn me just like my parents, so why bother. The only person I could lean on was Michelle. We did have each other, which I am eternally grateful for, but we were terrified and afraid of what would happen to me and us and what was to come. The waiting was the worst part.

After a week or so, I had heard nothing. It was quiet. Too quiet. Like the quiet before a storm. I had not heard from either of my buyers and I thought this was a good sign. Maybe, the cops would stop with them and not dig any deeper? Oddly, I started breathing a sigh of relief and feeling like the worst was behind me. Maybe the police were not coming for me? Maybe, I had gotten lucky and dodged another bullet? And maybe I was going to get out of this like I had so many times before?

I was still in possession of a large amount of drugs that I could sell, so I started thinking of ways I could get connected and start moving product locally. I had a false sense of security that everything was going to be ok. I tried to tell myself that this was just another bump in the road that I would somehow get out of.

Another week went by. It had now been two weeks after the original phone call, and everything was still quiet. Still no word from my buyers up north and that was the way I wanted to keep it. Blindly, I really started telling myself that I had somehow survived this scare. I was finally starting to exhale and felt like I was going to be ok. It was going to be ok I kept telling myself. It always worked out for me, so why would it not this time. Yes, this was a pretty big bullet to dodge, but I had dodged a lot of bullets of all shapes and sizes. I knew someone was looking out for me, but I did not know who or why. Reality had not yet kicked in, but it was about to become clear. My world was about to really get turned upside down.

CHAPTER 8

There Will Always Be A Knock at the Door

❧

We all must pay for our mistakes at some point. We do not get away with sin or crime forever. At some point, like it or not, judgment and punishment come knocking at our front door whether in this life or the next. This judgment and punishment look differently for all of us. For some, it is a spouse or a parent or the IRS or a business partner. For me, it was several layers and departments of law enforcement agencies.

As I look back on my life and specifically the events that transpired over the months that followed, there are so many moments that God was protecting me, and I did not see it. Isn't that always the case? When we are in the middle of the storm, we do not see the hand of God protecting us or Jesus sleeping in the boat beside us. Our faith wanes or, even worse, we do not even have faith. We do not even recognize Jesus or God's presence beside us and with us. Hopefully, though, when we look back, we should be able to realize and point to these moments recognizing that God was there.

I have many moments like this, but three really stand out to me as moments where the only explanation I have twenty years later, is that God intervened and saved me. He had saved me so many times before and since, but these three, if they had not happened exactly the way they did, would have resulted in me spending a large portion of my life in prison. I would not be the man I am today. I would not have the family I have and the life that I am so blessed to have lived.

The first of these three moments came about two weeks after my initial call from my buyer up north.

It was now mid-June of 2000, and as I stated before, at this point I had started to feel comfortable again. I was trying to move on and kept telling myself that I was in the clear. Just another near miss. But deep inside, I knew something still was not right. As much as I wanted to tell myself everything was going to be ok, some part of me knew it was not. Several times in the weeks leading up to this, I had sensed that I was being followed while I was driving. I kept telling myself that I was just being paranoid. Maybe I was, or maybe I was not. But something kept telling me I was not. Some voice kept telling me that I was not as safe as I thought I was.

I remember one night falling asleep in the spare bedroom of our apartment. It felt like I had just fallen asleep when I suddenly awoke very abruptly. I realized it was still the middle of the night, but it felt like something or someone had woken me up. I had been in a deep sleep, probably the first time I had slept in weeks, so it took me a minute to get my bearings and realize where I was. Then, suddenly I became filled with fear and terror. Someone was in the room with me! I could sense it. I immediately scanned the room, but no one was there. I could not immediately see anyone in the room, as it was pitch black, but I knew someone, or something was there with me.

As I struggled even more to get awake, I could more clearly sense a presence in the room and immediately sensed that something bad was about to happen to me. And then as if there were someone standing next to me speaking to me, I heard a voice very clearly say,

"Pack up all of the drugs in the house and get them out of here immediately!"

I was so overwhelmed and startled that the adrenaline was exploding in my body. I knew there was no one physically in the room with me, but someone had spoken to me and was continuing to speak to me. I was completely terrified, but I kept hearing the voice repeating that I was in danger and that I needed to get all the drugs that were in my house out of there immediately. I am not sure how many times the voice repeated itself, but it was enough for me to receive the message it was trying to convey. And then suddenly, the presence and the voice vanished. As quickly as it had come, it had gone away. It was gone and there was complete silence.

I did not sleep the rest of the night. My mind was swirling with thoughts and racing with emotion. Who had spoken to me? Did I really hear a voice? What should I do? I knew the answer to all these questions. Inexplicably, I knew that it was in fact God who had spoken to me. I knew I had heard a voice. And I knew that I needed to do what the voice said and get the drugs out of my house. The next morning, I packed up all the drugs and took them to a friend's house. I knew now that the police would be coming for me. The question was when?

Two days later in the middle of a weekday afternoon, there was a knock on our apartment door. Michelle was at work and I was home alone. I immediately knew that this was it. I knew without looking through the peep hole what was waiting on the other side. I opened the door and calmly let a dozen or more undercover cops, along with a K-9 dog, in to search our apartment. There were members of the Tampa Police Department (TPD), New Hannover County, NC sheriffs (NHCS) and Naval Criminal Investigative Service (NCIS) present. They searched the house and found nothing. I was allowed to call Michelle and tell her what was happening. That was a fun call to make!

Thinking back on it all, it seems so surreal. I was interrogated and questioned for I do not even know how long. I gave them nothing. They finally read me my rights and cuffed me. This was and will forever be the LAST time I am handcuffed and arrested. I was transferred to the Orient road jail where I was to be held until I was transported to North Carolina.

So, let me explain how the night, two days earlier, when the Spirit of God had told me to get the drugs out of my house was truly a miracle. At the time, I did not fully understand what was going on. What I mean is I did not know what I was being charged with and by whom. My two buyers had been arrested in North Carolina jointly by the NHCS and the NCIS. They had rolled over on me and provided details to these departments about who I was and how our operation had been run. The NHCS had enough information to arrest me, so they contacted the TPD to fill them in on the situation and obtain the TPD's blessing to come to Tampa and arrest me.

The TPD had never even heard of me. My name had never come up in any of their local investigations because I had mainly worked out of state. They were completely in the dark as to who I was or the operation I was running in their backyard. As a matter of fact, very few people locally knew the scale of my operations or what I was doing.

The TPD were a little shocked and embarrassed, from what I was told, that this was taking place under their noses and they did not know about it. So, they agreed to let the NHCS and NCIS come to Tampa to arrest me, but they wanted to be involved in the arrest. The TPD was hoping that I would have drugs at my residence, so they could arrest me also. And here is the miracle!

I did not have any drugs in my apartment because I had moved it all two days earlier after I had heard the voice in the middle of the night. If there had been drugs in my apartment when they came to arrest me, I would have been arrested on trafficking charges in Florida. Then I would have been facing charges in multiple states and they would have been able to possibly prove that I had been trafficking drugs across state lines, which would have resulted in Federal charges. I was already facing a minimum of 51 years in prison, as you will read later, so additional charges in Florida and possibly Federal charges would have been disastrous. The outcome of my story would be completely different. I would not be writing this story today. The legal issues I would have been facing would have been exponentially worse.

I did not understand or fully see God's intervention at the time, but now that I know how the entire story plays out, I know with absolute certainty that it was God's hand and voice that delivered me. It was God who spoke to me that night and told me to get the drugs out of my house immediately. This is the only explanation. He alone knew what was to come and he alone could save me.

My first night in jail was memorable to say the least. I was in a holding cell next to a guy who was having serious withdrawals from heroin. He screamed and moaned the entire night. I did not sleep a wink. I laid there, suffering from my own withdrawals, and tried to piece together how I had gotten to this point. Questions swirled around in my head, along with the screams of my neighbor. The uncertainty of my situation and what was to come were maddening. I was filled with a fear and terror that are hard to put into words. How bad was this going to get and how long was I going to be in jail?

The next day I was transferred to a prison block within the Orient jail. Most of the guys in my block were serving sentences for various lengths of time and a variety of charges. I was fortunate to get roomed up with a guy who served as a custodian at the prison, so he had a little more leeway with the guards and inmates. This was where I would spend the next two weeks. I just waited. I was a prisoner to my own thoughts. It was the longest two weeks of my life.

My first Sunday in jail was Father's Day of 2000. As I finished writing this book on Father's Day 2020, it was twenty years ago today. I had told Michelle to call my parents and explain to them where I was and what had happened. The call did not go well. My family was ROCKED!!!!!!!! I cannot even imagine what they were thinking or how devastated they were. I asked Michelle to ask them if they would take a collect call from me on this day. As a father now, I cannot even imagine how this made my dad feel. Getting a call from his son from jail on Father's Day. My and my family's relationship was so bad at this point and my and my dad's relationship was even worse, so I had no idea how it would go.

I remember that day preparing for the call to them. It was not easy. I was filled with so many different emotions. There was a lot of anger and bitterness in me towards my dad and my family. All the arguing and anger had taken such a huge toll on all of us. There was also a ton of unforgiveness inside of me for the previous ten plus years of my life. A very large part of me blamed them for my circumstances. In my mind, it was all their fault for how they had raised me and then pushed me away from them. They had done this to me, or more specifically my dad, and God had done this to me too.

There was also a lot of fear inside of me. I truly felt like I might never get to see them again. I might never get the chance to forgive and ask forgiveness. I might never get the chance to be hugged and be held by them, which is all I really wanted at this point. I just wanted to feel safe and secure again. I wanted to be loved and make all of this go away. There was also still an enormous amount of love inside of me for them. It had just been covered up and buried by years of hostility and animosity. Before, I had not remembered nor did I want to remember any good times with my family, but now the few good times I could remember were all I was holding on to. Buried under all the crap was still a foundation of love and happiness. It just had not seen the light of day in so many years that I did not realize it existed. It took something happening that was so catastrophic for myself and my family to finally start chipping away at the layers of hate and anger and unforgiveness.

And that is what my arrest and the phone call I was about to make started to do. All the pain that we had suffered together and were about to struggle through for many years was about to be set on the path to redemption in one five-minute phone call. That is all it took.

I will never forget this call for as long as I live, and I know my dad feels the same way. It was truly a turning point for me and my dad and the years of damage that had been done to our relationship, but we did not realize it at the time. I remember starting off the call by telling my dad that I was in jail. The tears started flowing. I know for most men, including myself, that would be an extremely hard thing to have to tell your dad on Father's Day. Then, I told him;

"If you don't start loving me unconditionally as your son and stand by my side—I never want to talk to you again!"

I do not know why I said that or why I became immediately angry with him given my circumstances. I could not think of any other way to start our conversation. We had not spoken in months and the last time we did speak, our conversation ended with a terrible argument when a lot of hurtful things were said to each other. All I can say is that in that moment I was tired of all the anger and hostility we had shown each other over the years. I was tired of how we had treated each other and what had become of our relationship. The only thing that I wanted and needed at that moment was the unconditional love and support of Dad. But I did not know how to express that because we did not know how to communicate with each other.

For the first time in many years, I truly needed and wanted my dad to just hold me and love me and tell me that everything was going to be ok. Inside I was a scared little boy who had screwed up, but I did not want him to punish me or judge me or chastise me. I had made a mess of my life and for the first time in my life I was truly terrified of what might happen to me. I just wanted him to tell me he loved me and that he was going to be there for me no matter what.

And that is what he did. I do not remember his exact words, but he told me he loved me, and he told me he would be there for me. Love had finally started to win the battle for our hearts. Love finally started to shine on the darkness that we had built into our minds and our relationship. Love finally started to chip away at all the negative words and emotions. Unforgiveness and anger were finally starting to lose their grip on us. We both started crying and the rest of the conversation is a blur. I tried to keep it together so the rest of my inmates would not see me crying, but I could not. There was so much emotion flowing out of us because of the damage we had caused each other and for the lost years that we could not get back.

Looking back, my getting arrested was and will always be one of the greatest things that happened to me. I truly mean it. It changed my life for the better forever. It created a story that only God could fulfill and use to touch others' lives. And it changed my relationship with my family, especially my dad, and with God towards eternal love and healing. I will share some quick thoughts here. Parents please do not wait until your grown child is calling you from prison on Father's Day to tell them that you love them unconditionally and that you will support them no matter what. Do not wait until it gets this far because it just might be too late. By no means am I encouraging parents to enable children, both big and small, to continue making unwise and unhealthy choices. But do not push them away and cast judgment on them for their sins. Let God handle that. Our job as parents is too mold them and transform them into young adults using the blueprint that God has provided us with and the very foundation of this blueprint is unconditional love and mercy.

I stayed at the Orient Road jail for just shy of two weeks. Michelle came to visit me a few times along with a few of my friends. It is funny that when I was out partying and having a good time, I had all the friends in the world, or so it seemed, but the moment I got locked up in jail, I felt alone and abandoned. There was no communication from the police. All I knew is I was being held until I could be extradited to North Carolina. I did not know how long that would be, so I just waited.

Michelle was able to secure an attorney for me in North Carolina. This case was a big deal in Wilmington and Camp Lejeune so through a series of events and phone calls, she was able to secure the attorney that kept coming up as the "best" attorney for my case. After Michelle had secured the attorney, he shared with Michelle the gravity of the situation. I remember her visit while I was still in Tampa in jail when she shared with me the potential prison term I would be facing. It was a minimum of 51 years in jail with no chance for parole.

Wow. Hearing that I could face 51 years in jail completely knocked the wind out of me. My world was ROCKED once again!!! I immediately broke down in tears. Reality had just slapped me in the face, and it stung really, really badly. Unfortunately, at the time, North Carolina had extremely strict laws and punishment for drug offenses as severe as mine. They had minimum term limits for each charge and I was facing three charges with a minimum of 17 years attached to each.

Looking back, I could not fully wrap my mind around this. I was in complete shock. We never think about the consequences of our choices until it is too late. The thoughts of my future and what I had gotten myself into haunted me the rest of the time while I was at

Orient. It just did not seem real. I was finally extradited to North Carolina via bus. This was a six-day journey that was extremely uncomfortable to say the least. I, along with 40 or so other prisoners, were shackled at our hands and feet to the floor of the bus. We slowly moved up the east coast stopping at prison after prison along the way to either drop off or pick up prisoners. By the fifth day, I was moved to a van, along with a handful of other prisoners to take us into North Carolina. I did not have any socks on so the shackles around my ankles had rubbed to the point that my ankles and feet had begun to swell. I tried to tell the guards, but they were indifferent. I could barely stand.

By the fifth night, we stopped at a jail for the night. I was able to shower and sleep on a cot. My feet were so swollen that I could not feel them anymore. They were purple, and I could barely walk. I remember accidentally catching one of my feet on a piece of metal, and it cut my skin. Yellow puss came shooting out. The rest of the prisoners with me told the guards who called their medical staff to examine my feet. They said that I had come close to possibly losing my feet. Thankfully, I did not have to wear cuffs around my ankles the rest of the way, but this was another bump in the road along my journey.

Finally, I arrived in Wilmington. My time here moved quickly, or so it seemed. After I was booked, I immediately met with my attorney. He filled me in on the details of the case and what my next steps were. I was going to meet with the NHCS narcotics division, along with a member of the NCIS, to be interrogated. His advice to me was simple; tell them everything and cooperate unconditionally. Apparently, my two partners that had set me up had not done the same and it had rubbed the police the wrong way. So, my attorney said that the police were already on edge and that I needed to answer every question honestly and willingly. Trust me, he did not have to tell me twice. The reality of the situation by this point had finally sunk in. I did not know what good, if any, it would do, but I knew that my future was in the hands of my attorney, the police, and the judge; and it was time for me to start taking responsibility for my actions. A few days later, we all met for me to be questioned. It lasted hours, and I told them everything they wanted to know. I held nothing back, and I could tell that they were receptive to my honesty.

And here is the second miracle I want to point out in my story that shows God working on behalf of Michelle and me.

Unbeknownst to us, the TPD had not gotten over the fact that they did not get an arrest out of this situation. So, even though Michelle had not sold drugs and had nothing to do with my operations, they were planning on going to Michelle's work and arresting her in her office out of spite and as a way to use her as leverage against me. Michelle was just starting out her career at the time at a global CPA firm in Tampa. She is still with this firm and is now a partner. Her career and this firm have blessed her, our family, and me greatly over the years. If she had been arrested in her office, even if on no other grounds than suspicion and as a way to get to me, her career there would have been over before it had even started and who knows where she and our family would be today. The TPD were waiting on the NHCS to start my interrogation. If I was anything less than 100% compliant and cooperative, they were giving the TPD the green light to arrest her.

I remember about 15 minutes into my questioning one of the officers making a point to get up and leave the room to make a phone call. I did not realize it until afterwards that he had called the TPD and told them that I was 100% on board and not to arrest Michelle.

I remember sensing the same presence in the interrogation room with us that day that I had sensed in my bedroom the night I was warned to get the drugs out of my house. I remember clearly thinking that it felt like someone else was in the room with us. But unlike that night a month ago in my bedroom, this time the presence was not one of warning or fear or terror. This time it brought peace and calm. It brought clarity and wisdom to everyone in the room.

I look back now and know that God's presence was in that room with all of us. There was a peace and clearness with me and all the police that should not have been there given the circumstances, but it was. I remember the hours of conversation with them being lighthearted and even jokingly most of the time. They kept saying to me that they could not believe that an educated, all-American looking kid like me could ever get wrapped up in something like this. The head of the narcotics division said that when he closed his eyes and listened to me, I reminded him of his own son. God clearly had His hand on this situation and was finally starting to steer my ship away from the rocks of destruction and towards a path of salvation and healing.

Unfortunately, I was not out of the woods yet. When the investigation finally concluded two years later in 2002, more than eighty enlisted marines and sailors and ninety-nine civilians were arrested and convicted. This turned out to be one of the largest military drug investigations in the recent years and to this point I was the top player that had been arrested in the pyramid of this operation. Yes, I had been fully cooperative and honest with them, but someone needed to be held accountable; and I was it. I was still facing a 51-year prison term and had little to no options of how to avoid this. My back was against the wall.

The NHCS working with my attorney brainstormed on next steps and came up with the idea of me "rolling over" on my supplier in Tampa in order to potentially reduce my sentence. This meant I had to work with them in setting him up. This was a hard decision for me to make. Extremely hard. I did not want to pass the burden of my own actions on to him, and more significantly, I was deathly afraid of him. I did not know who he was "connected" to, but I knew he was "connected." These were not the kind of people that you just rolled over on and walked away from easily. I would be putting my family and those closest to me, along with myself, in great danger by making this choice. But I also was driven by a strong sense of self preservation, which is inherent under these circumstances. I did not want to spend the better portion of my life in prison, so I agreed to help them.

The tricky part of the plan was we needed someone else to help us. We needed someone who was close to the situation that would be willing to help me and that could get close enough to my supplier under the circumstances to set him up. The only person that fit this bill was Michelle. I was going to have to ask her to sacrifice her own life and her own well-being in order to save me. That was a hard call to make.

I never dreamed that I would be putting her in a situation like this. But the only way to ensure our future together was for her to do the unthinkable. We contacted her and walked her through the plan. Even after hearing that she would be putting her own life in danger, she agreed, which shows the true strength of her character and her devotion and loyalty to me. For those who know her now, you know that she chose to do this with more strength and courage than most, if not, all the rest of us would have. She was and is a rock!

The NHCS devised a plan for us to "quietly" return to Tampa. There we collected the remaining drugs that I had given to friends to hold. Michelle needed to contact my supplier and have him agree to meet her. At the meeting, she needed to get him to agree to take the drugs from her. Michelle also had to agree to wear a wire for their meeting. The NHCS worked with the TPD to set up the operation.

We all met at a hotel in Tampa, which they had set up as the base of operation. Michelle made the call to my supplier, and he reluctantly agreed to meet her. I cannot imagine the emotions she felt during this whole sequence of events. I know the emotions I was feeling and can sense them now as I write this. Thankfully, Michelle was and is much stronger mentally and emotionally than I am.

The drugs were loaded in her car and off she went. I was filled with so much fear and anxiety. So many thoughts and questions swirling around in my head. What had I done? How could I put her in this position? What if this did not work?

I remember sitting in the hotel room with the officers as we listened to her through the wire. The bottom line for me was if she could get my supplier to take the drugs from her then the police could arrest my supplier. If this happened, then the NHCS would be willing to get the charges and sentence reduced and the TPD would be willing to potentially not seek charges against me. If the plan failed and my supplier did not accept the drugs from Michelle, then I was it. Meaning, I would face the full brunt of the law and there would be little to no room for negotiation with the DA and the judge.

While we waited, I could feel the anxiety and tension building inside. The officers were all joking around, and I remember a couple of them making light of me possibly spending the rest of my life in jail. Reality just kept punching me in the face. Michelle arrived at the meeting spot and started talking with my supplier. They spoke for a few minutes about me and what was going on with me in North Carolina and then she smoothly transitioned into the drugs in her trunk and started asking him what he wanted her to do with them. She told him that she did not want them and that he should take them. He immediately sensed danger and started trying to get away from the conversation. He wanted nothing to do with them. As he started to try to get away from the situation, she began to plead with him to take the drugs. She swore that she did not want them and was planning to flush them down the toilet if he did not take them back. She said anything and everything she could think of to get him to take the bait, but he would not bite. Finally, one of the officers turned to me and said something to the effect of, "Guess you're it. You're going to be spending the rest of your life in prison."

It felt like the earth beneath me shook. I was helpless and knew it was over. My entire life had come down to this one moment.

In my head for the first time in a very long time, if ever, I cried out to God to help me. "God if you are there, if you have ever been there with me, Please! Please! Help me now!" I was screaming this in my head. This could not be it. This could not be the end. "PLEASE GOD! HELP ME NOW!" I was begging and pleading in my mind to a God that I had turned my back on many years ago. The same God I had so often claimed had left me and was never there for me, I was now begging for mercy and compassion.

And this is when the third miracle happened.

As I prayed and begged in my head for God's help, at that same moment, my supplier either said enough or agreed enough with what Michelle was saying, without ever agreeing to take the drugs, that the police decided to move in and arrest him. He never even touched the drugs.

It was quick. The parking lot immediately filled with police. They arrested my supplier and swooped in and got Michelle. She was finally safe and now I just had to wait for her to get back to the hotel.

This was an extremely sobering time of reflection for me. The adrenaline to that point had been continually pulsing through me for over six weeks. I could barely control my thoughts and emotions. But what happened while I waited for her was I started to reflect on all the events of that six weeks. It was all flashing through my head.

So much had gone on that I never had time to slow down to wrap my head around it. I never had time to think about what I was going to do next. I never could allow myself to hope that I could possibly get through this and what I would do if I did. For the first time in a long time, long before I was arrested, it felt like my future was not predestined and all because my past was finally starting to be wiped clean.

When Michelle got back to the hotel and I knew that she was safe, for the first time since I had received the initial phone call in late May, I felt a huge sense of relief. I still had no idea what was to come, but I sensed that this had been a turning point in the mess I had created and in the rest of our lives. God's hand had been present in the situation and He had been beside Michelle and me every step of the way guiding and protecting us. At the time, we did not know how to recognize it, but looking back now I fully understand His role in all of this.

For the first time in a long time I finally exhaled.

CHAPTER 9

When It Gets Worse Before It Gets Better

～

For me, the hardest part of my journey started now.
I know that seems hard to imagine given everything that Michelle and I had just been through, but it is true. The main reason is I had to start my life over again. I had to figure out what I was going to do with my life. I had to attempt to start rebuilding and mending relationships, especially with my family. I had to clean myself up and not go back to the old life from which I had just been given a reprieve. This was hard. Addiction is hard. And it was creeping back into my life. I just couldn't shake my addiction.

Also, I had to face the fear and terror of what would happen to Michelle and me once my supplier was out of jail. This was an enormous burden! We had to go into hiding. It was hard, but we did. We had to completely change our lives and seek as much anonymity as the circumstances would allow. All these separate uncertainties were frightening and overwhelming, but combined, made for an enormous challenge that Michelle and I had to face. Many times, I was not sure we were going to survive. But we did. Somehow.

Michelle and I did the only thing we thought we could do. We hid. We completely pulled away from the rest of the world. We walked away from all of our friends and the life that we had lived for several years. We simply did not know what else to do. We were terrified of everything and everyone. We had no idea in whom to trust, so we trusted no one. Unintentionally, we burned all of our friendships. Close friends who wanted to support us, but did not fully understand what we had been through and what we were dealing with were left behind wondering what had happened. I became a terrible friend if I were even a friend at all. We just did not want those closest to us to get hurt. And being close to us seemed like a recipe for getting hurt. We lived in as much terror and isolation as we possibly could. It is hard to describe the level of fear that we were dealing with. It felt like we were constantly having to look over our shoulders waiting for something bad to happen.

We moved into another apartment together and tried to put as much distance between ourselves and the rest of the world. We only had each other. No one else had been through the battles we had faced. It was just Michelle and me. We did not realize it at the time, but the distance was what we needed. This was part of the journey we had to face together. This was part of the unwritten sentence for the crimes that had been committed and the life we had lived. To this day, I am eternally grateful for this. It made both of us stronger as individuals and most importantly, as a couple. I know that no matter what, I can ALWAYS count on Michelle. We have been through the fire together and we survived. Our very survival depended almost solely on each other for many years and as a result, it melted into each other. Our souls were welded together by our pain and our past.

During this time, Michelle continued to work at the firm she had been working at for a few years and I got a job in the lending industry. Our routine became very automated. We worked and then came home. We rarely talked or spent time with anyone else. We felt judged, flawed, and unforgiven by everyone else. My job was less than demanding and the hours were basically come and go as you wanted. Michelle, on the other hand, was working long hours. This left me with a lot of time alone sitting in our apartment to think about the mistakes I had made. The only thing I could do to make this go away was drink. I drank heavily every day of the week. I did not know how else to make the pain go away. The voices in my head that were constantly reminding me that I was a terrible person and a failure were only quieted when I was intoxicated. Also, I still partied pretty heavily on the weekend. The only difference was I would stay home and party instead of going out to clubs or parties. I just could not break the cycle of depression and addiction that I was falling deeper and deeper into. Life started to feel more and more devoid of meaning and purpose.

In October 2000, Michelle and I got married in Jamaica. Originally, we had a big wedding planned with all of our friends. It was supposed to be the party to end all parties. That would never happen. We had to quickly change our plans after I was released. We had planned on honeymooning in Jamaica, so we decided to make it a destination wedding. The only people we invited were both of our parents and each of our sisters. That was it. Just a quiet ceremony on a gazebo that hung out into the Caribbean blue water. It was a great day. An amazing day! The first and last that Michelle and I had for a while. For one day, we were able to try to forget about our past and try to focus on a future that had not been written yet. All of us tried to enjoy it, but there was still this unspoken tension with our family. We felt loved and forgiven for a day, but this felt temporary.

I wish I could tell you that I recognized all of this and found a way to seek God and completely turn my life over to Him. But honestly, I did not even know how to do that. Here I was again like I had been after the first time I was arrested without any clue how to turn my life completely around. I knew going to church was a place to start, but that faded fast. I did not have people around me to guide me to Christ and to help me take the proper and necessary next steps.

My life continued to feel like a turbulent mess for many years to come. I battled depression, drugs, and alcohol. I felt like a ship without a rudder for many, many years. Sure, I had a bachelor's degree in Accounting, but I didn't know what to do with that and besides I had convinced myself that I was an epic failure and that no one would ever hire a convicted felon, especially not one who had been convicted of the crimes I had.

The one lone bright spot is that I can thankfully share that I never sold another drug again. Everything I had been through had been enough to make me realize that I never wanted to turn to that life again. I never wanted to put my family or myself through the pain and drama of what we had been through. For the first time, I fully appreciated my freedom and did not want to jeopardize that. I know many of you think that sounds a bit redundant, even idiotic. Many would say that, of course you would not want to go through all of that again. You're right, but it is not that easy. It is never that easy. The lifestyle does not just let you go. It always tries to pull you back just when you think you are finally free. And the pulling always feels stronger than the last time you tried to walk away.

Living in the aftermath was extremely difficult and proved more challenging at times than I was prepared to handle. The damage I had done was significant and catastrophic in certain situations. As I mentioned previously, I battled with addiction long after my arrest. It was my only way to escape. It was the only way I knew how to numb the pain and the fear. It felt like my only real place of joy. There was so much emptiness and void left inside of every inch of me. I believed that I had completely destroyed my life and my future. I was empty again and even more so than before.

What I did not realize is all these struggles are a part of the lesson that I needed to learn. It was not supposed to be easy. Fixing and cleaning up my mistakes was not meant to be fun. If it were, I would have never learned from them. I needed to realize that I was never going to fully change or grow or realize God's full potential for me if I did not have to suffer and fight and claw to repair my mistakes. Yes, the damage seemed immeasurable and the process to fix and repair it took many years, but that was the point. That struggle to survive, and the constant feeling of emptiness showed me just how flawed I was and how much more I needed God's love and forgiveness to fill the void inside of me. Jesus' sacrifice for my sins was the only thing that could truly bridge that gap.

This is a lesson that everyone needs to realize. This is where we all have a choice. Are we going to let our past sins and transgressions and our inability to forgive ourselves enslave us for the rest of our lives, or are we going take the mess we have made and use it for a purpose and a calling that is intended for good? Are we going to use our screw ups to help heal ourselves and those around us?

Like most people, for many years, I chose to allow Satan and unforgiveness to bind me and hold me in a dark place. But slowly over the course of many years, I allowed God to heal this addiction. I allowed God's hand to slowly work in my life and consequently the chains started to break away.

CHAPTER 10

When the Prodigal Son Finally Returns

❧

The final chapter of my legal saga was to be sentenced. I did not know what this would entail, but I again, unexplainably at the time, had a peace that it would be ok. I had been arrested in June of 2000 and my sentencing was scheduled for February 2001. There was a lot that happened during this time. A few highs, but even more lows.

As I discussed in the previous chapter, Michelle and I got married in October 2000. This was an amazing high! But most of the rest of my life was just one great valley. Lows became lower and lower during this time. I hated my job, if you can even call it a job. Inside of me was a constant battle. My head was a mess. My sleep was a mess. As a matter of fact, I did not sleep. How could I close my eyes for even a moment? I knew if I did, that would be the exact moment when something bad would happen. If I even let my guard down for a split second, that would be the second that the unthinkable could happen. I felt like I was constantly drowning.

The sentencing day finally came. A lot of the emotions that I had pushed down deep inside started to come back. For eight months, I had allowed myself to look into a wide-open future. I had allowed some small measure of hope and joy to enter my life. I was not yet taking the steps to change my day to day existence, but I started to hope that someday it would be better.

Miraculously, I never served another day in jail. I was convicted of three felony conspiracy to traffic drug charges and in that small moment in time, it felt like all of the charges had been forgiven and washed away. The DA, NHCS police, and ultimately the judge saw potential in me that I still did not see. For some reason, they agreed that I could do better. My attorney shared with me that my interaction with them had convinced them, that of everyone involved, I was the one who needed to be spared. They felt like I had the most potential to change and give back to society and to make a difference.

I hope I have.

I wish I could show them where I am now. I wish I could thank them for letting me have the chance to turn my life around and be able to live the life I have led. I wish I could show them the family I have raised and the man I have become. I hope that I have lived my life to the fullest, so that they will someday know that their grace and mercy will be eternally rewarded. I hope that I make their sacrifice worth it by sacrificing myself.

I was sentenced to a few years' probation and community service. Another truly amazing miracle. I had gone from facing a minimum sentence of 51 years in jail to no jail time at all. I can only imagine if I had gone to jail for 51 years how my life would have been different. I would not have Michelle or my kids or the amazing life that God, and He alone, has provided for me. I would not have my relationship with my family, which had been missing for so many years. I would not have the ability to touch others' lives by sharing the pain and victory of my past. I am here today only because of God's grace, mercy, and hand guiding every step of my life. God once again saved me!

And who was the one person who had come on the final stage of this journey with me and was there after the judge levied my sentence and granted my freedom?

My dad.

Just eight months earlier, our relationship, if you can call it that, was in shambles. But here we were just a father and his prodigal son hugging in the middle of a courtroom in North Carolina. A father who truly loved his son, but somewhere along the line had forgotten to tell him. A father who had tried his hardest to love and support his son and to raise him to be a God-fearing man, but had forgotten to take the time to teach his son how. A son who became so blinded by anger and hatred that he did not see his dad standing right beside him trying to help. A son who thought his dad did not love him and had left years before because he was too immature to recognize the truth. There we stood; the two most unlikely people in the world to be standing there holding each other were doing just that. The last two people you would have thought eight months earlier would be letting forgiveness win over unforgiveness were actually forgiving.

My dad was there for me to love me and to hug me and hold me through my tears.

He was there telling me he loved me and that he would be there for me the rest of my journey in life. I had been gone for so long and had gone so astray that the threat of losing me and never having the chance to share in my life turned his heart of stone into a heart of love.

The prodigal son had finally returned, and his dad was there running towards him to meet him and welcome him home.

CHAPTER 11

The Long Road Back to God

❧

O f course, my journey was not over at this point. Far from it. As I shared earlier, when I reflect on my life, this part of the story was the hardest part. Cleaning up our mess always is. And that is what I had done. I had made a mess of my life. I had made a mess of every single relationship I had. And repairing the damage was harder than creating the damage.

And the one relationship that I felt like I had damaged the most was my relationship with God.

As I thought about God and where I fit in with Him, I simply viewed myself as disgraced and unlovable. Blemished and unforgivable. Flawed and worthless. How could God love a sinner like me? How could I truly be forgiven for all my failures and mistakes? Would God really forgive me for mocking Him and blatantly turning my back on Him? Could God really forgive the mistakes that I made or were they just too big? The answer to these questions always felt like a **NO**.

So, I struggled. Struggled to find a job. Struggled to break free from my addictions. Struggled to completely mend my many broken relationships, especially with my dad. And most importantly, I struggled to have a relationship with my heavenly father.

I just could not or did not know how to repair my relationship with God. I cannot explain why it was so hard for me to turn to Him for forgiveness. I know I cannot be the only one that feels this way.

I just cannot explain it. In retrospect, it was a lot easier to ask my dad and my family for forgiveness than it was to ask God for forgiveness. Now that I am older and my relationship with Christ is so much different and more mature, I look back and think it should have been the opposite. God is the easiest one to ask forgiveness from because He is the only one capable of truly loving us unconditionally and forgiving us without remembrance of the past once it is done. He forgives us no matter what. No strings attached. No lingering bitterness or animosity. But I just could not get there.

What was creating this block in my heart? What was causing me to be unable to lay my baggage and past at the foot of the cross and walk away? Why couldn't I forgive God or be forgiven by Him?

Guilt. Shame. Unforgiveness towards myself. Anger with myself. Feeling worthless and flawed. The list goes on and on. All of these were holding me back from truly being free of my past and from mending my relationship with the One who truly matters. I had created a wall so huge and so thick that nothing in my power could break through it. *So, how did God finally break through? How did I mend this relationship that felt so scarred?* I can honestly say that this was a long process. I was stubborn and rebellious and ashamed.

As I shared earlier, without a doubt, I would compare my journey to Jonah from the Bible. I spent years of my life running away from God. The only difference between Jonah and me is it only took Jonah one time in the belly of a whale to change and turn towards the path that God was leading him down. For me, it feels like I have been in the belly of 50 whales. And every time one spit me out on shore, I got up, turned my back on God, and walked right back to where I had come from, but God was patient and was still working in me. He was still writing my story. He knew I was not ready yet, so He protected me from harm and from my past, and just allowed me to continue to trip over my own feet knowing that someday I would see His light and seek out His forgiveness and guidance for my life.

I floundered and stumbled through life for about five years after my arrest. Every day felt like a battle. I worked in mindless jobs that I hated. But I did not know what else to do. I had to earn a living. This, along with still battling addiction, made for an extremely depressing and toxic combination. It was at this point that I truly hit the lowest point in my life.

I hated my life! I hated waking up every morning with the thought of having to do the same thing I had done the day before! I hated looking at myself in the mirror because I hated the person looking back! I hated who I was, who I had become, and what I had done! I was stuck in a never-ending cycle of depression and addiction. On the inside, I was screaming so loud that I thought everyone could hear me, but there was nothing coming out. I was not alone, but I felt alone.

Michelle did everything in her power to help me, but it never felt like enough. I am not sure she even knew how depressed I was. Many times, I asked myself, *"what was the point of going on?"* And the only answer I could ever come up with was Michelle. I had hurt her so much for so many years and she always stood by me. She was always there to clean up the mess I made. She was always there to save me from numerous situations of varying circumstances. She had always been the lifeline that got me out of tough situations. So, the only reason I could ever come up with to keep living was that I did not want to hurt her or leave her with a mess to clean up that might be too much for her to handle. I was not keeping myself alive because I wanted to or because I felt like my life had any value; I was keeping myself alive because of her. She saved me and this time she did not even know it.

The miracle though was I did not realize it, but there was still a miniscule amount of hope buried somewhere deep inside of me. In some remote corner of my spirit, there was still a tiny sliver of hope that no matter how hard I tried to get rid of, it still held on. And that is all that I needed. That is all any of us need. It only takes the tiniest amounts of hope to win out over the darkness. That is the beauty of hope. Your entire life can seem hopeless and filled with darkness, but if you even have an inkling of hope left, it will prevail if you allow it.

And that is what I finally did. I finally started focusing on that tiny speck of light in the darkness. I finally allowed myself to feel hope. I drew a line in the sand and said no more. No more feeling sorry for myself. No more letting my past hold me back. No more allowing addiction to handcuff and weaken me. No more looking in the mirror and hating every fiber of the person looking back at me. It was time to change. It was time to move on and to start to forgive myself and seek out the absolute forgiveness of those I had hurt. It was time to start the next chapter in my life. It was time to hope.

Finally, at the age of 30, I went back to college and finished my 5th year Accounting degree. I sat for the CPA exam and passed on the first try. I searched for a job in public accounting, but this was an enormous challenge. Someone with multiple felony drug trafficking charges is not who CEOs typically want to represent their firm. It was not easy convincing others that I was a "changed" man, especially those in a white-collar industry where appearance, transparency, and a strong moral compass are a foregone conclusion. But again, it never is easy, and it is not supposed to be. I had to answer serious, future-impacting questions from a lot of different people, including potential employers, regarding my past. Unfortunately, I heard no more than yes during this process. Many times, I cried and wanted to give up. I constantly felt alone and like a total failure. I was still battling with massive amounts of depression. But somehow, I never gave up. I still had hope.

I continued to battle and push forward even when the mountain I faced seemed too big to climb. I walked away from addiction, without ever looking back. My will to survive and to make something out of my life became so strong that I did not need my vices anymore. And thankfully, I was eventually given an opportunity and hired by a public accounting firm. Most of the people I worked with had no clue about my past, and there were times I heard jokes from them about how someone who had broken the law could never work in the industry we were in. Boy, would they have been surprised if they knew about my past.

Did I enjoy my job? No. I actually disliked it very much. But this was all part of the journey. This was all part of the process of cleaning up my mess and proving to myself and those around me that I could change. I was not completely walking in step with God's final plan for my life, but He was starting to guide me. Every part of this process was intended to show me that I could overcome my past and that I was not unlovable and unforgivable as I had convinced myself I was over many years. I was not actively seeking God's guidance or advice, but I was starting to seek His forgiveness and approval. And this was all it took to slowly start to break down my wall.

During this time, Michelle and I got connected with a small local church, for which we are eternally grateful. The message of this church was different from any we had ever heard before. It was focused on God's grace, love, and most importantly, forgiveness. I remember one of the mottos they embraced was, "No perfect people allowed." This was contrary to the way I viewed God and the teachings of the many churches I had been in before. The message was clear; we have all screwed up and we are all sinners. We all have a past that sometimes feels unforgivable. Michelle and I were instantly drawn to these teachings. They were so relatable and for the first time, we both felt accepted by a church and more importantly, by God. We started attending more and more regularly and God started chipping away at our past. He started healing the scars and wounds and replaced them with love, mercy, and forgiveness. The journey was still slow for both of us, but especially me. Because of what I had learned as a child about God, I continued to have a hard time fully placing my trust in God and believing that he could save a wretch like me. But He knew this, and He never turned His back on me, and He never stopped loving me. He was patient and knew that I still needed to grow and experience some bumps and bruises.

And then the unthinkable and a truly amazing miracle happened for Michelle and me ...

—

CHAPTER 12

God Saved Me for The Last Time!

❦

As I mentioned in the beginning, God loves surprises. And this surprise He used to save me.

At this point in our journey, Michelle and I had been together for almost twenty years. Before this point, we had never really considered having children. We were just too busy living our lives the way we wanted in a selfish way. But God, just like my grandmother, was tired of waiting for me to become fully vested in changing my life and following Him. So, He intervened, and no I do not mean it was an immaculate conception. I mean He knew what it would take to finally get my full and undivided attention.

It was September of 2009 and Michelle and I were planning a long trip to Aruba, our home away from home. We loved to travel and always had a lot of vacation time to use, so our trips were normally a minimum of two weeks at a time a couple times a year. Life seemed great. It finally felt like I had turned the page on so many dark chapters in my life. Michelle and I had well-paying jobs, we loved to travel and could afford to do it and we were not really tied to any other major commitments in our lives. Could it get any better?

But life still felt very empty. There were times when I still felt there was a significant void in my life. Michelle and I had each other and I constantly told myself that this was enough, but I knew that was not the case. The Holy Spirit was working in me. It was making me uneasy with the direction of my life and the choices I was making. I remember thinking and telling Michelle on a trip a year earlier that we should think about having kids. I think we both just chalked the declaration up to one too many tropical drinks. So, like the many other times before and since, when the Holy Spirit was trying to guide and direct me, I chose to run and hide. I guess I thought if I stayed hidden in a little ball in the most remote spot in my mind, God would eventually forget about me and go away.

He did not.

Hiding seemed to be working for me until a few weeks before our trip on our way home from church Michelle announced,

"Do you think we have been running from God and not doing what He wants with our lives? Do you think we are supposed to have kids?"

Not fair God! Now you are going to use Michelle? I was stunned and relieved all at the same time. The selfish Marcus, the one still holding on to what he thought was best for his life, was shocked and a little frightened by these words. But the new Marcus, the one God had been working on for many years since He freed him from a life in prison, was immediately filled with peace and joy because I knew this was the right path for our lives.

Considering starting a family was a real turning point in my and Michelle's faith and relationship. For the first time in either of our lives, we were finally being receptive to the Holy Spirit. We were both finally hearing God's voice clearly on how we should start living our lives. As we drove home, we both agreed that this was what God wanted for us and that we should follow through with this. The Holy Spirit had been working on both of us for so long and this was the first time that we both willingly agreed to follow God's direction for our lives. The light inside of us had started getting bigger.

We agreed that once we got back from our trip that we would just see what happened. We were not going to do anything special to get pregnant, say, lock ourselves in a closet. We decided to just go about our normal routine. We agreed that we would eliminate all "safety nets" and leave it in God's hands. I even remember us saying those words over and over again that we were going to leave it in God's hands. We truly did mean it. But at the same time, we would also say that it might not happen. If God did not want us to have kids, then we would not have them. Our selfish nature was still holding on, but not for long.

And then the unthinkable and a truly amazing miracle happened … Michelle got pregnant!

On December 22, 2009, eight weeks after we got back from our trip, we found out that Michelle was eight weeks pregnant. A week after that, we found out we were having twins. *Ok God, message received!* I immediately thought to myself!

Michelle's pregnancy went smoothly for the first six months. We were excited about the next steps in our lives and what having not one, but two children at a time, would bring. It felt like most parts of our lives were going smoothly. Nothing but smooth sailing from here until the delivery date. But that is normally when unexpected bumps in the road of life happen—when we least expect them. Michelle had started feeling a little off one day and felt like something was not right, so she went to her doctor to be checked out. The doctor examined her and told her to go to the hospital to be examined further. Michelle called me and we met at home before going to the hospital. We were not worried; we never are, so we took our time. When we got to the hospital and checked in, something seemed off. The hospital staff immediately rushed her back into a room and said that they had been waiting for us. What we did not realize and what had not been communicated to Michelle was that she was in pre-term labor. When they got her into a room, it was discovered that she was having contractions and was not aware of it. Her contractions were six seconds apart. She was twenty-six weeks pregnant and both babies were extremely tiny, so neither baby was more than a pound at this point. The doctors and nurses were immediately rushing around trying to save the babies' lives. They advised us that if they came at this point, there would be a slim chance that one, or either of the babies, would live. It was total chaos. At one point a doctor stopped and told Michelle that there was no way that she would be able to delay the babies' births and that they were coming and we should expect the worst.

Neither of us slept much. It seemed like we were living from one minute to the next, not knowing what would happen. We were overwhelmed and the waves seemed to be once again crashing in all around us. Amazingly, this was another one of many turning points for our lives and our faith. You see, amid all of this chaos and noise, our initial reaction for the first time in our lives when being faced with a situation that seemed too big for us, was not to trust and put our faith in our own abilities or wisdom or put our faith in someone else. No. Our first response was to pray and ask God for the strength and protection that only He could provide. For the first time in our lives, we turned to God. We did not realize it, but our faith had started growing enough that we could think of nothing else except asking God for help. And that's what He did. After three days in the ICU, Michelle was moved to a regular hospital room. She was far from out of the woods still, but she was slowly improving and was starting to understand how to control the contractions and to keep herself settled amid all of the stress. The doctors very callously told her that she would be lucky if she were able to keep the babies inside her for a week. I laugh now as I think back on this. I'm not sure why this one doctor in particular continued to announce to

Michelle that she was not going to be able to save the babies lives and kept pounding the point that they were only trying to give her a few more days, so the babies could develop more. Whatever his reason, his pessimistic view was the best thing for us similar to waiving a red flag in front of a raging bull's face.

Michelle is *extremely* competitive. Michelle does not lose at anything. So, by telling her she would not be able to save the kids' lives or be able to keep them in long enough to guarantee their health, was just the motivation she needed. After a week, the doctor decided to move her into the long-term bed rest wing of the hospital. The doctor advised that she would be there on permanent bed rest until she gave birth and would not go home before then. She politely asked the doctor how long she had to be there until she would be allowed to go home. He laughed and told her if she could make it another seven weeks until her thirty-fourth week of pregnancy, then she could go home.

She said, "Then, I'll see you in seven weeks when you release me." And that's what she did.

She never complained or was upset to be there on bed rest for that long. Every day she woke up and thanked God for one more day in the hospital as it was one more day the babies were safe and for His plan to save the babies' lives. She knew that God wanted her there and that by her being there, the babies would be healthy and be born with no issues. For this, she thanked God for her circumstances, not begrudged Him. We were both finally seeing how putting our trust in God to handle situations like this gave us a sense of peace and understanding that He was in control and that everything would be fine. At thirty-four weeks, Michelle was discharged from the hospital. God had won over modern medicine. She was finally able to go home and knew now that when the babies came, they would be alive and healthy. With God's strength, she was able to do what the doctors said was the unthinkable. God had again performed a miracle in our lives.

One week after being discharged from the hospital, on July 4th, her water broke and our children were born. I sat alone in the hospital lobby that night waiting to be called back to the delivery room. As I did, I was thanking God for protecting us and getting us to this point in life. I looked back on what could have been and what now was and thanked God for giving me one last shot ten years earlier and allowing me the freedom to be able to have this moment. God knew what we needed to strengthen our faith and point us to Him.

The birth of our children, Michael and Mykala, was finally what got our attention and turned our lives towards God. This is when Michelle and I began to not only talk about making wholesale changes, but truly made them and stayed committed to them. For the first time, we truly started following God's path for our lives. Our twins' birth was just another of many miracles in our lives. Not only did Michelle and I recognize that it was God's hand at work in our lives, but more importantly, for the first time we recognized and gave God the glory for performing a miracle in our lives. After all the times that God had rescued me or saved me, this was the first time where I saw that and fully gave God the credit for it.

Michelle and I realized that if we did not want our children to make the same mistakes and live out the same life that we had, then we alone were responsible for guiding them away from those mistakes and pitfalls. We realized as parents, we could not tell our children to not do what we had done and yet continue to live our lives as we wanted. We had to be the example. We realized also that we could not tell them to have a relationship with God and to live life in accordance with His teachings and guidance and yet not have a flourishing relationship with Him ourselves.

The selfishness of our lives started to be washed away. We started reading our Bible more devoutly and praying individually and as a couple. We became more involved in our church by serving and joining small groups. Tithing and giving back to others and most importantly God became essential to our lives. We started our own couples' devotion that helped us through the hard six months after our twins were born and have helped us many times since. And as we met with our devotional group, God started to bless us more and more abundantly in every aspect of our lives. As we more rapidly turned our lives over to God and started living out His teachings in our lives, we started experiencing more and more of the healing and peace that only He can provide. God started showing me that all the hurt and the pain of my past was not meant to be a stumbling block for my future; it was meant to be a tool to guide me and use for others. He revealed to me that my pain and suffering was not intended to bind me, but to free me and to help those around me.

Life still was not easy. It never is. But as we grew stronger and stronger in our faith, our lives and our relationships became easier and easier.

Several months after their birth, we both tried to go back to work. Two working parents in public accounting is extremely hard to do. My heart was not in it. I hated my job and it was reflected in my work and attitude. In April 2011, for the first time in my life, I was fired from a job. My firm was making layoffs and I had made it through the first two rounds, but I did not survive the final cut. I was devastated, but completely relieved. I remember calling Michelle to tell her and fearing her response. As I told her the news, her response completely blew me away.

She said, "This is great! I have been praying that you would lose your job. This is God's way of telling you that it is time to move on, but you weren't listening."

What? Her response was amazing, and I knew immediately that she was right. Again, this is what I needed. God was trying to direct me and help me, but I was too stubborn to listen, so He intervened. But unlike every other time before when I had faced failure, this time, I did not allow it to consume me or enslave me. Quite the opposite. I knew that God wanted me at home with my children. He wanted me to be a stay at home father and to take care of everything at home, so that Michelle's non-work world would be as stress free as possible and she could focus on her career. Also, I knew that God had a greater path for me in mind and that someday His plans would be revealed to me.

God saved me for the last time.

CHAPTER 13

Just A Father and His Son

∽

As I stated earlier, how I viewed my dad paralleled how I viewed God and vice versa. In my younger years, I viewed them both as angry and unloving. As I felt judged and rejected by my dad, I similarly thought that God was also judging and rejecting me. If my earthly father, who was flawed and born into sin just as I was, did not accept me, then how could God, who was perfect and without blemish, accept me?

At twenty-six, as I sat trying to pick up the pieces of my life, I remember thinking every minute of every day that there was no way that either my dad or God would ever truly forgive me. I had shamed and hurt them too much. I was too much of a failure living deeply in sin. I was unlovable and unforgiveable.

I could not have been more wrong.

It took me a long time to finally realize this. It took years more of addiction and depression until I finally started to change and accept the love and forgiveness of my dad and God. Every time I took a step in the right direction, I would hear the voice of guilt, shame and insecurity. These were always standing in my way trying to destroy me, and it worked for a very long time. There is no defining moment that I remember repenting and finally coming back to God. I don't have a day on my calendar that I can look back on and say that, on this day, I fell to my knees and begged God for forgiveness and He made me whole again. What I do have, though, are many days like that. Hundreds of days over the many years that passed after my last arrest that I fell to my knees and begged God for mercy and forgiveness. Hundreds of times trying to be freed from my past and begging for the pain to be gone. It took me a long time to finally figure this out, but God had forgiven me the very first time I had asked for His forgiveness. That was it. I never needed to ask for forgiveness again. But I struggled to see it. I remember one night, several years ago, being alone in the parking lot of our doctor's office with my dad. I am not sure what triggered this, but I broke down and cried with my dad and asked him for his forgiveness for our past and for the pain and suffering that I had caused him. I had asked and been forgiven by him many times before, but I once again needed to ask him for it. He cried with me and finally said,

"Marc, I already have forgiven you, and God has already forgiven you. But the problem is you haven't forgiven yourself."

Most of my life I had spent believing that my dad and God did not love me and could not forgive me, but I was wrong. The Bible is full of verses that describe God's mercy and forgiveness. God forgave men and women who committed far worse sins than mine. God states in Isaiah 43:25 that He is the one who blots out our transgressions and He is the one who remembers our sins no more. The bottom line is both God and my dad did love me. They both were able to forgive me. They were able to stand by me when life seemed insurmountable. They were able to look past my mistakes, hurt, and pain and say that they would be there unconditionally for me. They were able to stand by my side and support me even when what I had done was wrong and sinful and to tell me they would be there for me. They were able to hug me and tell me it would be all right.

That Father's Day that I called my dad from jail and he told me he would be there for me no matter what, he really meant it. And that was where the forgiveness began, and the bitterness started to crumble. That is where we stopped being enemies and started to heal our relationship. We finally started putting our differences aside and just started loving and forgiving.

As I write this today, it is Father's Day, twenty years to the day after I made that call from jail. And I can tell you without hesitation that my dad is one of my best friends. No, our relationship has not been and will not ever be perfect, but he was there for me as I picked up the pieces of my life. After that Father's Day call, he has supported me without condition. No, his love is not perfect like our Heavenly Father's, but it is perfect for an earthly father. I am grateful for his love and my family's support. As I look back, there are three distinct moments for me that reflect the healing that has taken place in our relationship and his love for me.

First, Michelle and I got married in October 2000 just four months after my arrest. We had a big wedding planned, and our honeymoon was supposed to be in Jamaica. Given everything that had happened, we chose to cancel the wedding and get married in Jamaica. Only my parents, Michelle's parents, and our sisters attended. My dad performed part of the ceremony. This is very special to me and him. I do not think any of us had ever imagined that our relationship would have changed so rapidly in so little time, but it did. Four months earlier, my dad wanted nothing to do with me, and here we were on a gazebo in the middle of that beautiful blue Caribbean water with my dad performing part of our marriage ceremony.

Again, God used my arrest and pain to bring us together. He used my sins and past to bring healing to my family, Michelle, and me. If I had not been arrested, my dad and I would have never reconciled. I would have never felt convicted to ask him for forgiveness for all the challenging times I had put him through. God used great suffering in my life to bring about great healing for myself and family.

The second instance of the healing in my and my dad's relationship was my sentencing in February 2001. As I mentioned before, just my dad and I made the journey together. We drove up together as a father and a son. How amazing is this! Eight months earlier, we never wanted to talk to each other again, and here we were, going to face my future together. This was God using terrible events to heal us and to further His kingdom. We do not ever fully understand it when we are in the eye of the storm, but God has a plan for us. He has a reason for allowing us to go through the storm.

The night before my sentencing, my dad and I went to a movie together, which is something we had not done since I was very young. I will never forget the movie we saw, *Cast Away*, with Tom Hanks. My dad and I both cried several times throughout the movie. I know we could both relate to the storyline of a guy being stranded on an island all alone. I know I had felt like that many times in my life, especially with my relationship with him and God. And I am pretty sure my dad had felt that way with me and his life also.

I did not appreciate it at the time, but as I look back now as a father myself, I realize that Dad was there for me. All the pain, anger and confusion that had been seeded into our relationship, all the hatred and rebellion that Satan had tried to use to destroy us—none of them mattered. What mattered was that Dad truly loved me and wanted to protect his son. My father truly cared about me and was willing to stand by me. God was using this situation to heal us and to make wholesale changes in our lives.

The third and final reminder of Dad's love for me came after the birth of my children. When they were only a few months old, one day Michael was not feeling well. Of course, any parent of an infant knows that there is no way for them to communicate this. So, as parents we become worried. Michelle and I sat on our couch with our babies lying between us. I held Michael continually for hours not wanting to let him go. All I could do for him was hold him and love him.

I realized in that moment that my dad had probably done the same for me. Yes, there were probably many days when I did not feel well as a baby and he had held me, loved me, and consoled me. He had held me the same way I was holding Michael because he loved me so much that he did not want to let go. I had not realized it as a teenager and young adult, but my dad had always loved me. No, neither of us communicated this the way we should have or showed love unconditionally to each other for most of our lives, but at the very core of his existence, my dad had always loved me and would have sacrificed anything for me the same way I am willing to do for my son and daughter now.

Conclusion

❧

One of the greatest lessons from my story that I want to convey to anyone reading this is HOPE.

So many times, I did not see it or feel it or even think it was there, but it was. Through all the valleys and the lows, I somehow always had hope that tomorrow was going to be better. I cannot explain it, but as I look back on my life, I can see it. I realize that the hope I had wasn't there because of me or because I wanted it to be; it was there because of God. It was there because God allowed it. He put it there. He knew that my life was meant for so much more than I was making out of it. He never gave up hope for me and he planted that seed of hope inside of me.

We all have this hope. Some of us are just on different parts of our journey, so it looks different. Some people have already discovered God's hope. Their lives are not perfect or painless, but they have discovered the peace that only God can provide. When the storms come, and they will, they immediately turn to God and know that He is there with them, even if the waves seem too big. Even when they are surrounded by darkness on all sides, they have hope that tomorrow will be a brighter day. They know that the light that never goes out in the darkness is the light that only Jesus can provide. Their hope is not in this world and all of the brokenness that surrounds them; it is in the knowledge that this world is temporary and some day they will be free of it when they spend eternity with their Heavenly Father.

Many others, though, have not gotten there yet. They are still stuck in what seems like an endless valley. They are struggling to see that hope inside of themselves. They are struggling just to keep their head above water. They look at their past or their present and just do not feel loveable or forgivable. Their focus is on the enormity of their mistakes and not on the enormity of God's love and forgiveness. They only see the darkness inside of themselves. To these people, I say remember, "All have sinned and fall short of the glory of God." (Romans 3:23) Your sin and mistakes are no different from mine or anyone else's. It can get better and it will get better if you only take the steps away from the chains of your past and steps to move closer to Jesus, even the tiniest of steps, and the light and hope that He provides. I promise you that you can be forgiven. You can have hope.

My hope is that you will see my pain and my past and realize that we are all alike. We have all sinned and fallen short of God's grace and glory. No matter what the color of your skin or the language you speak or the baggage in your past. Sin is sin and we are all born into it. Forgiveness is for all of us with no questions asked. My hope is that no matter your circumstances, that you are able to relate to some part of my journey and use it as encouragement and support and an example of someone who has sinned greatly against God and been forgiven.

Yes, my story is one of great suffering and sinning against God. And yes, it is a story of broken relationships, unforgiveness, repeated failure, and depression because of my past. It is the story of a father and son that grew so far apart that forgiveness and redemption never seemed possible and almost did not happen.

Many, if not all of you, can relate to some part of my story.

But more importantly, my story is a story of redemption, forgiveness, hope, love, and grace. It is a story of healed relation-ships, success, and great victories in every part of my life. It is a story of a father and a son, who against great odds, were able to seek out love for each other. Finally, it is a story of a son's Heavenly Father, just like his earthly father, waiting patiently for his son to come back to him and to forgive the son and accept him with open arms when he finally came home.

While sometimes hard to imagine, your Heavenly Father is waiting for you to come home, but He is waiting for you to make that choice. If you choose to step away from your past and towards the light, it does not end there. You will have more decisions and challenges to face. If you are like me, you will continue to stumble along this path. Do not give up hope if you do. Look to God's strength to help answer the many critical questions you will likely be faced with.

Ask yourself:

- Will you let your mistakes weigh you down and enslave you for the rest of your life, or will you allow God to use your mistakes to benefit you and to benefit those around you?

- Will you allow yourself to use your past to help heal others who are downtrodden and burdened by regret and grief and unforgiveness?

- Will you do everything in your power to heal your broken relationships, which will allow you the freedom that you so richly deserve?

Only you can answer these questions. Only you can forgive and ask forgiveness. And only you can make the choice to focus on whatever sliver of hope is left inside of you instead of focusing on the darkness all around and let God change your life forever.

I will leave you with two verses that speak of the hope that God provides.

"We rejoice in our sufferings, knowing that suffering produces endurance, and endurance produces character, and character produces hope, and hope does not put us to shame, because God's love has been poured into our hearts."
(Romans 5:3-5)

"And your life will be brighter than the noonday; its darkness will be like the morning. And you will feel secure, because there is hope; you will look around and take your rest in security."
(Job 11:17-19)

Thank you for allowing me to share my journey with you.

My prayer is that this book saves just one person's life and that that one person is you.

Would you like to
Connect or Find Out More about
Our Mission
&
Outreach Programs?

Then please visit the official website:

www.**WeAreTheProdigal**.com

Mail to:
Marcus Clapper
7521 Paula Drive, P.O. Box 262767
Tampa, FL 33685

Acknowledgements

Writing this book has been one of the most rewarding and unique accomplishments of my life. I never would have imagined twenty years ago as I sat in that cell wondering how I had gotten there and what would become of my life that I would be writing a book about my journey twenty years later. It truly has been amazing to look back on all that I have been through and all that I have overcome and to realize that I am sitting here writing about it today. I cannot say it enough. I am eternally grateful to my Heavenly Father for allowing this to be accomplished. He is the author of this story, not me, and He deserves and is given all of the credit and honor. Without God, I would not be where I am today and I would not have the family that I love so dearly. He truly is an amazing God.

To my wife, Michelle, I give you all of my love and gratitude. How can I thank you and say that I love you enough? I can't. You have been so loving and supportive of me through many, many dark times. I really cannot believe that you stayed with me or that we survived all of the madness and the chaos of our younger lives. You have always been the strong and dependable one in our relationship. Thank God for that. I am so grateful for your strength and perseverance and tolerance of me. Thank for you for being an amazing wife and mother. Thank you for standing by me when I was all alone and for not giving up on me when you very easily could have. I am so grateful for the lives we have created together and for what God has done in each of us. I am also grateful for your love and support while I wrote this book. You encouraged me and had faith in me even though I again, did not see it. Thank you for all that you do for me and our family. You truly are and will always be my best friend. I have always loved you and will always love you forever.

All of my love goes to my son, Michael. In you I see so much of myself. I see all of your love and compassion for others and a selflessness that cannot be taught. I also see in you a chance to break the cycle of the Clapper father and sons' struggle to say and show love to each other. This is why I tell you that I love you many, many times throughout each day. I do love you and I want you to know that I will always love you no matter what. I am grateful for the second chance you have given me to do something with my life and to help you and others. I am thankful for the second chance that you have given me to heal the relationship with my own dad. I am eternally grateful for the boy that you are and the man that you will become. God has great plans for you. You are amazing and will do great things.

All of my love goes to my daughter, Mykala, who is the sunshine that shines on even the cloudiest of days. Your smile and all that is within you is greater than you will ever know. Your laugh and your joy have always lit up the hearts of everyone who has met you. Many times, your joy and the laughter in your heart has kept me going when I did not want too. You smile no matter what and I want you to never lose that. Do not let anyone take this from you. You are so very much like your mother and I am eternally grateful for this. You have her strength and emotional balance that few have. I want you to know that you can accomplish anything and everything that you put your heart and mind too. There is a greatness inside of you that you have not seen yet, but I hope and pray you will someday. You are perfect in God's eyes and mine. I love you so very much and you will always be my little girl.

To my dad, I say thank you. Thank you for your love and your forgiveness and your sacrifice for me and my family. I am so grateful that we have been given a second chance and that the early chapters of my life are not the ones that will eternally define our relationship. We have been through so much and you have been there when I needed you most. My prayer is that this book honors you and helps to heal you also. Thank you so much for standing by me and allowing me to leave and then accepting me when I finally came back.

To my mom, I also say thank you. You have given so much to me and our family. You constantly serve others and have sacrificed so much for me. You really are my biggest fan. I just never saw it. You believed in me when almost no one else did and you never gave up on me. Thank you for the sacrifices you have made and know that they were not in vain. My prayer is that this book brings a joy and peace to your heart that many times have felt out of reach for you. Thank you for all of your love and support.

To my sister, Evonne, I say I love you. Many times, you have been my polar opposite and that was a good thing. You are strong and amazing and grounded. You have given so much and many times, it has gone unnoticed or unrecognized. Thank you for all that you have done as a sister, sister-in-law, and aunt. Only God knows your path in life and no matter what that looks like, I will always be by your side. I know life can be challenging, but God has blessed you with so many amazing talents and attributes. I do not think that you fully understand the greatness that you possess nor have you fully embraced all you have to offer to those around you and the rest of the world. Always focus on the light you have inside and never let it go out.

A very special thanks goes to Dr. Jim Hogsed. You have helped and healed myself and everyone in my family for so long and so many times. You do not know this, but you were the first person who ever gave me real hope. I remember meeting you for the first time after I had been arrested. I was a mess physically, spiritually, and emotionally. You knew this, but you also saw and gave me a way to heal and repair the brokenness that I was. You were the first person to tell me I was fixable when I truly believed that I was not. Over the years, I have done many crazy things to my body and you have helped heal and rescued me when I was down and not well. I promise someday I will stop all the crazy cleanses and heavy working out. You truly are amazing. The talents and gifts you have been given will never be duplicated. Thank you again for all that you have done and the love and kindness you have shown myself and my family. You have been like a second father to me and over the years visiting you has been one of my favorite things to do. I honestly think I have made physical or emotional ailments up just as an excuse to drive to Fort Myers to visit you. I needed you and I will miss this. I know our paths are not done crossing, though, because you will have eternity to put me back together.

A special thanks goes to Toni Fairman. When our paths crossed eight years ago, there were still so many parts of me that were a mess. You saw this and were the first person that identified the emotional baggage I was holding on to and the affects that this was having on my health and day-to-day life. You were also the first person who was able to lead me down a path to healing this emotional baggage. If you had not introduced me to the emotional healing techniques that you did, my overall health and well-being would not be what it is today. This truly changed me forever. Thank you so much for all you have done for my entire family and for your patience and wisdom. You truly are amazing.

A special thanks goes to Pastor Hal Mayer. When Michelle was in the hospital on bed rest, you took the time to visit her. Your time and compassion left a mark on Michelle and me and your teaching as the lead pastor at the Church at the Bay allowed us to start mending and healing our relationship with God. Your motto of, "No perfect people allowed," left a lasting impression on us. It was the first time we had ever been in a church where we did not feel unloved and condemned because of our past. It was the first time we heard the message of a loving and forgiving God and not an angry, judgmental God. We honestly did not know church could be that way and it opened our hearts and our minds to a God we never knew existed. I also thank you for reading the first version of this book and telling me exactly what I needed to hear. It changed the course of my story and helped create the story I am sharing today. Your honesty, although not what I wanted to hear at first, was exactly what God wanted me to hear. You are a great man of God. Thank you.

I want to thank Stacey Wilson, the Editor of this book. I am appreciative of your time and effort in helping to transform this story into a book that is actually readable. You did an amazing job and I am truly grateful for your wisdom and insight in getting this done. I could not have done it without you.

Lastly, I want to give a special thank you to Eli Blyden and Racquel Piper. Being connected to you was truly the hand of God intervening at a point where I needed it. You coordinated and helped with every aspect of this process. You inspired me with your own testimonies and faith and the words of encouragement that you shared with me about my story were what I needed to hear when doubt was lingering in my mind. You both helped create this book and deserve much love and credit for everything you have done. I look forward to working with you on this in the future and if I ever write another book, you two will be the first people I call.

About the Author

Marcus is a stay-at-home parent who wears many hats for his family. He serves as the personal chauffer for his ten-year-old twins, Michael and Mykala, family travel agent, family financial advisor and planner, personal chef for Michelle and the kids, and family comedian. He serves at his church, loves to travel, loves Aruba, loves to workout, loves sports, and loves the Miami Hurricanes.

Marcus is just an average guy no different from anyone else reading this book. As the old saying goes, "he puts his pants on one leg at a time just like everyone else." He is not a polished author, a famous celebrity, or really anyone all that important, which is why Marcus feels it is so important to share his story.

He has made many mistakes just like everyone else and was given a second chance to do something with it and that is what he is attempting to do.

Made in the USA
Middletown, DE
12 June 2021